Why Not Change the World?

See the Invisible, Change the World

From Atheistic Scientist to President of God's University

May 2006

Young-Gil Kim, Ph.D.
President
Handong Global University
Pohang, Korea

Unless otherwise indicated, Bible quotations are taken from the HOLY BIBLE, NEW INTERNATIONAL VERSION®. Copyright © 1973,1978,1984 by International Bible Society.

Handong Global University (HGU) is an Affiliate Institution of the Council for Christian Colleges & Universities (CCCU) headquartered on Capitol Hill in Washington, D. C. (www. cccu.org)

Handong Global University: www.handong.edu
The Office of the President: ygkim@handong.edu
Papyrus Basket Membership: gxlove@handong.edu, lahandong@hotmail.com

Author Contact : ygilkim7@yahoo.com

www.xulonpress.com

DEDICATED TO

Reuben Archer Torrey III
(1918–2002)
The founder of Jesus Abby in Korea in 1964,
who prayed for the establishment of
a genuine Christian university in Korea

RECOMMENDATIONS

"When former world-renowned NASA scientist and professor Young-Gil Kim left his prestigious professorship at the Korea Advanced Institute of Science and Technology (KAIST) to join the newly established Handong Global University to raise up future global Christian leaders, he experienced suffering, trials, and imprisonment; yet, his pilgrimage through Handong moved the hearts of millions."

~ Rev. Billy Jang-Whan Kim,
Former President of Baptist World Alliance,
and President of Far East Broadcast Company,
Seoul, Korea

"I first met President Young-Gil Kim and his wife, Young-Ae Kim, when they visited the LeTourneau University campus several years ago, and I became intrigued by their vision for Handong Global University. I caught a glimpse of the story of struggle and sacrifice that they and Handong had endured since its founding in 1995. Later, after visiting the campus in Pohang, Korea, I became deeply immersed in the faith journey of Handong and these two Christian leaders, as well as the students they served. Young-Gil and Young-Ae have been led and upheld by God through some of the most amazing experiences and challenges that Christian leaders can face. This book is a must-read for all who are looking for an example of God at work today through the lives of the faithful."

**~ Dr. Alvin O. Austin, President,
LeTourneau University, Longview, Texas, U.S.A.**

"Handong Global University is, indeed, God's university and consists of obedient and dedicated Christian professors called by Him. Through prayers, Handong has been able to educate and send out competent and honest global Christian leaders, despite the various perils, difficulties, and hardships that existed from the start."

**~ David Yonggi Cho,
Chairman of Church Growth International,
Senior Pastor of Yoido Full Gospel Church
(Seoul, Korea)**

Table of Contents

Preface.. xi

Chapter 1: From Atheistic Scientist to Christian
           Scientist.......................................15

Chapter 2: God Called Me as a Creation Scientist............33

Chapter 3: How the Lord Is Using Me for God's
           University...45

Chapter 4: Why Not Change the World?....................75

Epilogue.. 105

Appendix... 109

References.. 115

Papyrus Basket... 117

Preface

*I*n the brief pilgrimage of our life on this planet earth, we often face adverse circumstances and hardships planned by our Creator God. But as finite, mortal, and feeble creatures, we are unable to comprehend the providence of the infinite Creator God. From time to time in human history, God allows extraordinary visions to become reality.

This booklet is my personal story of how God called me, transformed me, and is now using me as His instrument. I was not a Christian until I worked at the NASA-Lewis Research Center, in Cleveland, Ohio, in 1974. As a natural scientist, I only believed in the existence of the visible material world only. My faith wandered from intense questioning to discovering the authenticity of the Bible. I went through a realistic intellectual exploration of scientific reasoning and evidences of faith. Along the journey, God transformed me from an atheistic scientist to the president of God's university. My testimony is a drama in which God has been the Master Director, and I have played the role of His servant, a vessel consecrated for His use.

God has led me along paths I could not see and by ways I did not choose. I was imprisoned for 53 days following a trial related to financial difficulties of the university. Through imprisonment, I came to realize that in all things, God works for the good of those who love Him and have been called according to His purpose (Romans 8:28). Indeed, God made me to be tested beyond my strength, and through the test, He made my faith grow and helped me fathom what His providence was. On this 21st century stage of God's drama, He has assigned me the role of creating a new Christian school, Handong Global University (HGU), which is the main title of the drama. It has been proven time after time that all the testing and hardships that I have had to endure have been for God's purpose of strengthening my faith and transforming HGU as a genuine university for Him.

Handong is a Christ-centered place of learning located in Pohang, a southeastern coastal city in South Korea. Since Handong opened its doors in 1995, God has brought about great progress very quickly, even through impediments and adversity that the school faced. Handong has continued experiencing unprecedented growth and accomplished remarkable achievements in academics against incredible odds, all through God's providence. During the past 10 years, I have learned lessons through my successes and mistakes and witnessed miracle after miracle. Through numerous trials, Handong has so vividly experienced guidance, love, and the supernatural provision of the living God, and has now firmly taken root as God's university, with the special global mission of evangelizing the developing nations in the far reaches of the world.

This is only my humble attempt to testify of some of the incredible things God has done through Handong — through my journey as an atheistic scientist to an instrument of God who has been called to oversee and administer the school as its founding president. I wish I had more words to convey my Christian testimony and to describe His wondrous blessings and workings at Handong. I hope and pray that you will catch at least a glimpse of the glorious adventure that has been guided and orchestrated by God from its very beginning.

I would like to acknowledge with deep gratitude my most sincere appreciation to Dr. Gaylen Byker, President of Calvin College in Grand Rapids, Michigan, and Dr. Alvin Austin, President of LeTourneau University, Longview, Texas, for their encouragement while I was imprisoned in 2001. For helping me to tell this marvelous story, I am greatly indebted to Professor Gihong Kim and Pastor Philip Kim, and others.

I would also like to express my deep appreciation to Alanna Boutin for correcting and editing this final manuscript while she accompanied her husband, Michael Boutin, to Handong as a visiting lecturer at the Asia Research Institute of Language and Culture (ARILAC).

Finally, I would like to thank my beloved wife, Phyllis Young-Ae Kim, for her endless prayers and encouragement whenever we have encountered impassable obstacles and impediments. This book is the companion book of *The Papyrus Basket — The School in the Wilderness*, authored by my beloved wife, Phyllis Young-Ae Kim, which was also published by Xulon Press Inc. in 2006.

Young-Gil Kim
Handong Global University
Pohang, Korea

xiii

CHAPTER 1

From Atheistic Scientist to Christian Scientist

Personal Introduction

I was born into a typical Confucian family in Andong, South Korea. Andong is located at the southeastern region of Korea, one of the most conservative traditional parts of Korea. The city became famous worldwide when Queen Elizabeth of the United Kingdom visited it several years ago. My ancestors trace back their roots from the fourth son of the last King of the Shilla Dynasty (BC57-AD935), and I am the 34th generation. My parents followed a scholarly Confucian tradition. They had four sons and four daughters. I was the youngest son, and my next older brother, who later became the founding president of Pohang University of Science and Technology in Pohang, Korea, was the most influential person in my life. He earned a PhD in nuclear physics at the University of Birmingham in England, and thereafter, worked at the Lawrence Radiation Laboratory, University of California at Berkley.

With my late father and late older brother in 1992 at our 340-year-old home, which has been designated as cultural property in Andong, Korea

I attended an elementary school in my hometown, my rural birth village. My father donated our inherited farmlands to the elementary school, where he served as the principal for 37 years. Throughout my childhood and upbringing, I was taught to believe in Confucianism. I was told to "revere the heavens and love man," which is a common saying in Confucianism. However, I had no clear concept of what the heavens really were. I was not a Christian and had never thought of becoming one before I got married. But God had a blessed plan to call me as a Christian through my marriage.

I graduated from the College of Engineering, Seoul National University, majoring in Metallurgical Engineering. Then I went to the United States to study and received my MS degree at the University of Missouri-Rolla. In 1969, when I was studying for my PhD in Materials Science and Engineering at Rensselaer Polytechnic Institute, Troy, New York, my parents introduced me to a bride in Korea. She was preparing to go to the States for her advanced graduate study after completing her MS in special education at the Ewha Women's University in Seoul. Following a blind date in Korea arranged by my parents, I sent her a marriage proposal, but I received an important response letter back from her. She wrote me that she was a Christian believer and suggested that a vital condition for our union would be my willingness to attend church once we marry. I informed her that I had never attended a church and had not ever considered becoming a Christian. However, I told her that if there were a "god" who would guide us after we marry, I would try to seek him. Then, I promised her that I would attend church once we became husband and wife.

I flew to Korea for our wedding on June 15, 1970, and then we returned to the United States. I decided to attend a church to keep my promise. Looking for a church nearby, I found an American Presbyterian Church ministered by the Rev. Robert Marsano in Troy, New York. That was the first time in my life that I had ever attended a church. But shortly thereafter, a tremendous obstacle confronted me. I had to translate the sermons for my wife. Since my English wasn't all that good at that time and I was not familiar with the Bible, it was very a difficult task for me. So, we moved to a newly opened Korean church in Albany, New York. I attended the church every Sunday, but I was basically just a churchgoer who enjoyed meeting other Korean people and friends socially, without much interest in the Gospel.

As an atheist, I believed that there was no relationship between God and science. Having majored in science and engineering, I naturally believed in materialism. When I heard the word "spirit," I thought it was merely a product of the human imagination. I definitely did not know and believe in a personal God. Because science deals with the physical, material world, it seemed inappropriate for a research scientist to believe in the spiritual world.

My Christian life did not begin in earnest until I was working at NASA in Cleveland in 1974.

Experimenting with high-temperature
aerospace alloys at NASA in 1974

NASA had been my hope and dream ever since I was a student, and I was very excited that my dream had been achieved during my career. But this job provided much more than the realization of my professional dream as it turned out later. At the onset of my career at NASA, I experienced a spiritual awakening and my eyes began to open through meeting with Christian friends there. Every Tuesday at lunchtime, a Christian fellowship and prayer meeting at NASA took place. I attended the meetings as a result of the guidance of a devoted American Christian friend by the name of Joe Mills.

Through the prayer meetings, I was challenged to learn about Christ, and I began to read the Bible. In the meantime, Christian friends at the Korean church had been praying for my Christian faith and growth. After each Sunday's worship, some close church friends and their family members gathered to share their faith with me and fellowship. I was greatly touched by their sincere attention to me.

Then I was faced with some important questions, like: *How can I believe in the invisible God as a natural scientist? How can I accept the Bible as the written Word of God?* Since the Bible is known to be the best seller in all of history, I wanted to find out what it was all about.

How Did I Come to Believe in God as a Scientist?

As an atheistic scientist, I thought that God and science had no relationship with each other. What is science? Science is about things. Science can be defined as the systematized knowledge of nature. Science is based on cause and effect reasoning, the so-called analytical method. Knowledge of science rests on repeatable experiments on things. As an atheistic materialist, I did not accept the existence of invisible spiritual or supernatural beings. I believed physical matter is the only ultimate reality. I assumed that everything in the universe, including life, could be explained in terms of matter and natural processes.

In the physical world, there are laws, orders, genetic information, design, and harmony. Scientific researchers seek to discover new phenomena, order, processes, and laws in the universe. Based on the scientific reasoning of cause and effect, laws are established by lawmakers and orders are produced by intelligence. But nothing can exist without the cause, and the First cause here is the omnipotent God. It is illogical to believe that something could begin to exist without an intelligent cause. A computer implies a computer maker. The most complicated human organ is known to be the human brain, which cannot come into being merely by an unintelligent evolutionary process of time and chance. God created the universe with all that is in it. This universe is the work of God and a product of His design. God is the one who created the world of science.

I was puzzled for a long time regarding the ultimate origin of the universe and searched for an answer. Scientific materialists have said that the universe is eternal, with no beginning and no ending. But surely that is unreasonable, based on the scientific reasoning of cause and effect. Modern astrophysical evidence indicates that the universe came from a single pinpoint of extremely dense hot plasma. The cosmic explosion of the pinpoint has become widely known as the "Big Bang." They say that physical space and time were created in that event, as well as all matter and energy from the "Cosmic Egg" in the universe. Then, the ultimate question is, Where did the primordial cosmic egg come from? What caused the Big Bang?

Science is based on cause and effect. There must have been the "First Cause" that brought the universe into being, since something cannot just come out of nothing. The universe requires a cause because it has a beginning. If there is a cosmic beginning, there must exist a cosmic creator. God is the Creator of the whole universe, and He is also the Creator of time. God is outside of time. God is eternal, with no beginning or end. God has always existed.

God is the invisible Spirit, and therefore, we cannot see Him with our naked eyes. Science only deals with the material world that can be felt through our five senses or detected by an instrument. Therefore, the existence of God is impossible to be proven directly by scientific experiments. However, there are many evidences for God's creation.

The Bible proclaims: *"For since the creation of the world, God's eternal power and divine nature have been clearly seen, being understood from what has been made, so that men are without excuse" (Roman 1:20).* *"Through faith, we understand that the worlds were framed by the word of God, so that what is seen was not made out of things which do appear" (Hebrew 11:3).*

Encountering Jesus' Miracles

I came to study the Bible for the first time in my life when I was 32 years old. Since the New Testament is shorter than the Old Testament, I started with it first. However, when I began to read the Gospel according to John, I confronted the first stumbling block to my faith — the first miracle performed by Jesus at the wedding at Cana in Galilee which He and His disciples had been invited to. When the wine ran out, Jesus asked the servants to fill the jars with water, draw some out, and take it to the master of the banquet. The servants did so according to Jesus' command. The result was quite astonishing to me — water turned into wine! (John 2:9) In an instant of time, the chemical equation was changed from H_2O to C_2H_5OH. So far, no nuclear fusion occurred in that room. How can pure water turn into wine instantly? What a miraculous event that was!! I told my wife that I would attend church, but I could not believe in the Bible. She was quite disappointed!! A few days later, I was told that some church friends started praying and even fasting for my faith. I felt so burdened, so I decided to take up studying the Bible again.

But then I encountered another great miracle. In John 6, Jesus had to feed a large crowd of people of around 5,000. Philip did not do anything, but Andrew took five small barley loaves and two small fish from a boy. Jesus asked the 5,000 to sit down on the grass. He then took the loaves, gave thanks, and distributed them to the seated people. Then, He did the same with the fish. The result was quite astounding!! When the crowd of 5,000 had had enough to eat, 12 baskets full of bread were still left (John 6:13). This event was even more astonishing to me than that of changing water into wine, because it contradicted and destroyed a very fundamental physics law of the conservation of matter.

Finally, I gave up studying the Bible altogether because I thought I was wasting my time. I thought I could publish more papers and invent more worthwhile patents if I spent more time in my research. However, after I quit my Bible reading, I lost all peace of mind. Furthermore, church members and friends at NASA continued to pray for my faith. My wife told me that I should just believe in the Bible. I wrestled with the question of God and started to read the Bible again and other books that dealt with science and religion.

The Bible was full of such illogical inconsistencies that it was too difficult for people like me to believe in it. It could have said that Joseph and Mary married and gave birth to Jesus, but why on earth did it say that Jesus was conceived by the Holy Spirit? *Who can believe such contradictions and unscientific reasoning?* I thought. If I accepted such miracles, what is the point of my scientific research?

Do Miracles Contradict Science?

As a scientist, I thought an event as a miracle when it does not conform with scientific or physics laws. Turning water into wine definitely contradicts physics laws. As a Christian scientist, how could I understand and accept it? We call something a "miracle" when it contradicts our common sense or cannot be understood by our human knowledge of the world.

Physics laws assume that no other natural or supernatural factors are interfering with the operation that the scientific laws govern. If I raise a stone with my hand, the law of gravitation acting on the stone is not violated or negated, but it is overcome by the greater force of my muscle. The stone cannot raise itself by its own force. However, if the stone were raised by a force invisible to me, I may consider such an incident as a miracle because I cannot see the force. Whether or not I can see the force does not affect the operation itself. An eagle flying in the sky does not violate or negate the law of gravitation. The gravitational force is overcome by the eagle's muscular force. But when the eagle dies, it will fall to the ground in accordance with the law of gravitation. The force of a higher dimensional world can overcome or override the force of the lower form of the world. The laws of the invisible spiritual world can override natural physical laws.

Miracles lie outside the realm of natural science where experiments take place based on our five senses. The acceptance of miracles requires a quantum jump or leap from the limits of our five senses into the spiritual realm. It depends on the level of one's perspective. There is no conflict between science and miracle. They are not really contradictory to each other; in fact, they are actually compatible.

God authored all scientific laws. He is above them and is independent of them. God can override them at will — though normally, He does not interfere with them. God is not limited by or confined to the universe. He created time, space, and all material in it. God is not a slave to scientific laws. He created them and is also the source of all life.

How and Why I Believe in Miracles

At last, I came to realize a total comprehensive worldview that covers all aspects of the world. God created both visible and invisible worlds as said in Colossians 1:16. Two different worlds exist: One is the visible, natural, material world, and the other is the invisible, supernatural, spiritual world. Science is concerned with the material, natural world while theology is concerned with the spiritual world. Scientific research is restricted to the domain of the material world. Many secular people accept and believe only in the existence of the visible, material world. Invisible does not mean something is nonexistent.[1] The invisible is invisible because it is in the spiritual world, which is outside the scientific realm.

When we analyze the human body from a scientific point of view, we find about 50 percent of its weight is water. The rest is bones and flesh. Bones consist of calcium and phosphorus, and flesh and muscles are made of carbon, hydrogen, etc. But is the human body really material alone? Can the material, natural realm explain the gamut of emotional pain or joy? It cannot. That is the limitation of science. Because the spiritual, invisible world is outside of the scientific realm, many people cannot accept its existence. How can we explain color to one who has been born blind? It is impossible!!

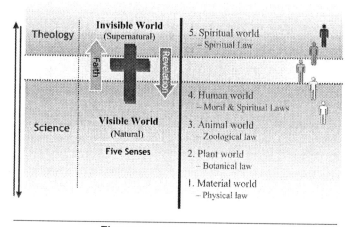

Five Different Worlds of Creation

Five Different Levels in the Visible and Invisible Worlds

There are five different worlds and God has ordained levels, order, and laws for each world and its various levels. Four levels are found in the visible, physical, natural world: The lowest is the atomic world, then, the plant, the animal, and the highest of these is the human world. The fifth and the highest level of them all is the supernatural, invisible, and spiritual world. As there are natural scientific laws in the physical world, spiritual laws exist in the spiritual world. God ordained the order and the laws for each world and level. For example, in the world of atoms, physics laws govern the rotation of electrons around protons. God created biological laws for living things, such as growth and multiplication. When He created man in His image, He gave moral and spiritual laws that were different than those He gave the animals. Human beings are created to be not merely physical, but are also moral and spiritual beings. The human soul consists of emotions, intelligence, and will. Furthermore, humans also have a conscience, which is part of their spiritual nature. Humans cannot live the good life without a conscience.[15] The major difference between animals and humans is the conscience. Since animals do not have a conscience, they cannot repent of sins.

The laws of the higher world contain and override the laws of the lower worlds. The invisible spiritual law is the highest law that governs the visible natural world. In geometry, lines consist of numerous spots, planes consist of several lines, and a solid cube comprises numerous planes. The visible natural world is the manifestation of the invisible spiritual world. The visible world is the phenomenon of the invisible world. Nature and super-nature are not two separate worlds, but different expressions of the same reality.[13] The invisible, spiritual world can be understood only by faith, *"By faith we understand that the universe was formed at God's command, so that what is seen was not made out of what was visible" (Hebrews 11:3).*

Since there are distinct levels or gradations in the created world, a lower level of life can never fathom a higher one. When animals observe the human world — people driving a car, operating a computer, flying an airplane — they cannot comprehend what is going on. These instruments are miracles to animals — but not to a modern man. A miracle to an animal cannot be a miracle to a human being. Just as a dog or a monkey cannot understand how to fly an airplane or operate a computer, can we not see that God's mighty acts are far richer and greater than we can ever comprehend? *"For my thoughts are higher than your thoughts, and my ways are higher than your way" (Isaiah 55:8)*. Turning water into wine is a miracle to human beings, but it is natural in the supernatural world when God intervenes. The acceptance of miracles in the Bible depends on the level of one's perspective, whether or not one believes and accepts the existence of the Almighty God, our Creator. The miracles Jesus performed are not the subject of scientific investigation or interpretation, but are powerful signs that Jesus Christ Himself is the Creator of the universe!! *"Through Him all things were made, and without Him nothing was made that has been made" (John 1:3)*. When we accept and believe that Jesus is the Creator, we should not have any problem in believing all the miracles He performed.

Searching for Biblical Truths

The Bible declares God as the Creator of the universe. *"In the beginning, God created the heavens and the earth" (Genesis 1:1)*. God is the Creator and Sovereign ruler over the world and history. God is the powerful intelligent Creator and has revealed Himself through His Creation. All natural worlds shout the Designer's intelligence. *"The heavens declare the glory of God: the skies proclaim the work of his hands. Day after day they pour forth speech; night after night they pour forth speech; night after night they display knowledge. There is no speech or language where their voice is not heard. Their voice goes out into all the earth, their words to the ends of the world" (Psalms 19:1-4).*

The first words of the Bible, "In the beginning, God created the heaven and earth" gave me some deep insight. While studying the first chapter of Genesis, I learned the Hebraic meaning of "creation" in Genesis 1:1. The word "creation" was the translation of "bara" in Hebrew, meaning from nothing to something ("ex-nihilo"). When the word "bara" becomes a verb in a sentence, the subject is always the Almighty Creator God. Meanwhile, the Hebrew word "Asa" means a transformation of the existing materials. Scientific research is concerned mainly with discoveries of new phenomena, order, and laws in the physical world. Scientists are not creating something from nothing. Technology is concerned only with the transformation of existing materials like what the "Asa" in Hebrew means.

The reality that God is a part of the Holy Trinity has been perplexing me for a long time. I could not understand the invisible spiritual reality through my visible scientific knowledge. So, I decided to believe, and then understand it. Through the Bible, I realized God's natural and moral attributes. God is transcendent and excels above all. God is almighty, omnipotent, infinite, and eternal. God is the Creator of universe. For me, the evidence of God as Creator was the starting point of my coming to faith in Him. God is my Creator. My faith has grown since 1971 to now in 2006 through reading many inspiring and apologetic Christian books.[1-17]

I looked for the credentials of the Bible and the witness of prophecies about Christ's birth, life, death, and resurrection.[2,3] The Bible is essentially a book of history with a single theme of Messiah, written by about 40 writers, covering about 2,000 years in different places and times. I searched and confirmed that hundreds of prophecies about the Messiah exist.[2] The probability of the fulfillment of these prophecies about Christ occurring by mere coincidence was thought to be mathematically impossible. Science is always built on human knowledge, and it cannot predict with absolute confidence what will happen in future events even one minute later. But in the Bible, *all* Old Testament prophecies written in a span of 1,100 years were fulfilled in the New Testament, proving that the words of the Bible were written by God's revelation. I acknowledge the difference between the Bible and worldly books. Best-selling author Paul E. Little's book, *Know What You Believe,* said that "It doesn't matter what you think of Play-Doh®, Napoleon, or Richard Nixon.[1] It does matter what you think of Jesus Christ." In the Bible, God unfolds His character, tells us where we came from, what our ultimate destiny is, and the purpose of our life.[12]

The Gospel of John, especially Chapter 1:1-14, gave me deep spiritual insight. *"In the beginning was the Word (logos), and the Word (logos) was with God, and the Word (logos) was God. He was with God in the beginning. Through him all things were made; without him nothing was made that has been made. In him was life, and that life was the light of men. ... He was in the world, and though the world was made through him, the world did not recognize him. He came to that which was his own, but his own did not receive him. Yet to all received who him, to those who believed in his name, he gave the right to become children of God ... The Word became flesh and made his dwelling among us" (John 1:1-14).*

The Word is not a merely concept. The Greek word for "logos" is used for intelligence, thoughts, reason, wisdom, communication, etc. In John 1:1, when the verse states, *"In the beginning was the word ..."* it is saying literally, "In the beginning were the thoughts and reasoning expressed."[11] This is a clear reference to the creation in Genesis 1:1 *"In the beginning God created the heavens and the earth."* God is seen creating the heavens and the earth. The heavens and the earth are the very expression of God's thoughts. His thoughts were made known in His creation. Thus, the heavens and the earth declare God's glory, because they are the product of how He expressed Himself in creating them: *"The heavens declare the glory of God; the skies proclaim the work of his hands" (Ps 19:1).* Creation reveals the Creator's glory. The ultimate goal of the universe is to show the glory of God. Everything created by God reflects His glory.

In John 1:14, "The Word (logos) became flesh and made his dwelling among us," the word logos here means Jesus Christ in His pre-incarnate state. Jesus Christ, the eternal God, became human being. Jesus Christ is the incarnate word of God.

A New Creature in Christ

The most dramatic and epoch-making event in Christian history was when the Creator God became a man, died on the cross, and resurrected after the crucifixion. The mystery of Christianity is the premise that God became a man. The reason why He became a man can be understood when we consider His characteristics, such as justice and love. Since God is justice, He cannot give tacit consent to sins or forgive sins without a penalty. *"There is no one righteous, not even one" (Romans 3:10). "For all have sinned and fallen short of the glory of God" (Romans 3:23).*

As there are physical laws in the physical world, there are spiritual laws in the spiritual world. If one jumps from a high building, he will die as a result of disregarding the law of gravity. Likewise, if someone disobeys spiritual laws, spiritual death will result. God is the Creator of the universe. He had an intimate relationship with the first human being, Adam. Sin is unbelief in God as the Creator (Romans 1:21), and the penalty of sin is death.

29

I wondered about what life and death truly are. Life is our interaction with our environment. A child is born with five senses and various bodily organs, each of which interacts with elements in the environment. The eyes see sights, the ears hear sounds, the lungs breathe air, and so on. So long as we are able to interact with our environment, we have life. Death is the failure of such interaction. When our first ancestor disobeyed God, man's relationship with God was broken, resulting in spiritual death for all of humanity. Man became separated from God. *"We are all sinners!" (Romans 3:23).* Why are we sinners? We commit not only numerous sins throughout our lifetime, but we are also born with sin. Our fellowship with God was broken due to our sins. But because of God's great love for His creation, He desires to restore His broken relationship with human beings.[9]

God wants to forgive the sins of human beings. His justice demands the payment of the penalty of our sins. There is no single person in all of human history who could pay off the penalty for his/her sins to satisfy the justice of God. Since it was man who sinned, animals or angels cannot die for the sin of man. Only a true human being, but one who was born without the sinful nature, was able to pay off the penalty for the human sins. So God devised a way in which He, Himself, could pay off the penalty for our sins. God became a true man without sin and died on the cross, thus paying off the penalty for our sins. The incarnation of God as the true man was the only way that He could forgive the sins of man.

After four years of marriage, I finally became a Christian, a new creature in Christ. It occurred Easter week in 1974 while I was working at NASA in Cleveland. I admitted that I was a sinner and acknowledged the penalty that was due my sins and the payment that God had made for my sins. Jesus Christ died in my place on the cross. I was born again by the Holy Spirit as a new creation in Christ. I humbled myself and knelt down before God to receive Jesus Christ as my Savior and my Lord. With painful contrition, I recognized my sinfulness before God. I confessed my sins before Him and asked with a crying heart for forgiveness. I cried out to the Lord and confessed that I accepted His suffering and death as His redeeming grace for me. Grace from heaven filled my heart, and I was a forgiven and newly born man in the Kingdom of God by the Holy Spirit. Since then, with a joyful and thankful heart, I have trusted Christ as my Lord and Savior and have been following Him wherever He leads me.

That wonderful day, I knelt down and prayed as a new member of God's family. "Dear Heavenly Father God! Thank you for saving me from my sins and giving me eternal life. Please lead me and use me as Your instrument to proclaim the Good News. Empower me with Your Holy Spirit to become a witness of Your Kingdom and Your glory." On that day, I was born again as "Nehemiah" Young-Gil Kim.

"To all who received him, to those who believed in his name, he gave the right to become children of God" (John 1:12).

CHAPTER 2

God Called Me
as a Creation Scientist

Meeting with Christian Scientists in Korea

I came back to Korea in December 1978 as a professor at the Korea Advanced Institute of Science & Technology (KAIST). When I was working there in 1980, I found new Christian relationships were waiting for me in the science research community in Seoul, where the various government research institutes were located. Many scientists who had been recruited from abroad had returned to Korea as Christians. Over 50 percent of the people in the research community were believers, the highest proportion of Christians in Korea for any group at that time. These Christian relationships paved the way for the birth of the Korea Association of Creation Science later.

In August 1980, the international conference entitled, "The Origin of Life: Evolution or Creation?" was held in Seoul, during the 1980 World Evangelical Congress. The conference was organized by the Korea Campus Crusade for Christ (KCCC). The keynote speakers from the States were

Dr. Henry M. Morris, the founder of Institute for Creation Research (ICR), Dr. Duane Gish, Vice President of the ICR, Professor Walter Bradley of Texas A&M University, and Dr. Charles B. Thaxton.

Presenting Scientific Creationism at the international conference

The conference organizer had been looking for a domestic speaker majoring in life science. They contacted a number of promising speakers, but they all declined the invitation, explaining that it would be awkward for them to deliver lectures denying the theory of evolution as life scientists. Y. Shim, who was then an MA student in chemistry at Korea University and an administrator of KCCC, came to see me. But I turned down his request, professing that I did not have enough professional knowledge as my major field was not life science. Mr. Shim did not take "no" for an answer. I, as a person who liked the phrase "ignorance breeds courage," said to myself, "If no one is willing to step up to the job, then I will consider it God's command and will obey."

Faced with a huge task suddenly, I diligently read through an armful of books on the origin of life published by the Institute for Creation Research (ICR) in San Diego, California, and other creationism groups. The two-day conference was held on August 13 and 14, 1980, to debate about the topic of the origin of life. Over the two-day period, more than 4,000 people attended the conference. I prepared my talk on "Scientific Views of the Origin of Life," and presented it at the conference. I was very tense because it was the first time in my life that I presented a paper to a large audience in a creation science seminar. But the seminar had attracted considerable attention because people had never heard the contradictions of evolutionism and the scientific evidences of creationism before.

After the conference in 1981, I was invited by numerous churches, Christian schools, universities, and organizations to hear my presentation on creation science. Faith in creation is the very foundation of a Biblical worldview and Christian education. That is why I decided to include creation science as a core course for all students at Handong Global University from the beginning in 1995. The following is a brief updated version of my creation/evolution seminar presentation. While I was writing this chapter of creation science, I learned much useful information about the subject and collected many useful quotes to increase my knowledge on creationism through numerous books.[4-11] I greatly appreciate my esteemed predecessors in the creation science field for their devotion and contributions, especially the late Dr. Henry M. Morris, the founder of the Institute for Creation Research in San Diego, California.

Scientific Views of the Origin of Life

There are two models on the origin of life: Creationism and Evolutionism.[4] The Evolution Theory is a naturalistic and mechanistic process, and it excludes the act of God. Its only main factors are time and chance. The Evolution Theory believes that basic elements such as hydrogen, nitrogen, and carbon, through a long period of time, accidentally reacted with one another and led to the formation of a single cell life form such as the amoeba. The amoeba, also through time and chance, transformed itself into a higher form of life. Thus, all living things are traceable to a common origin. In other words, the Evolution Theory believes that the amoeba is the "father" of the 1.5 million life forms on this planet.

On the other hand, the Creation Theory states that God created life with His intelligence and design, and every living thing was brought into existence by the acts of God.

Life Comes Only from Existing Living Life

Some people thought that living creatures can be produced naturally from nonliving substances. However, the famous French scientist and Creationist, Louis Pasteur, provided the first scientific evidence that living things are not produced from nonliving matter. In 1895, he conducted an experiment which countered the theory of the spontaneous generation of life. Pasteur's experiment showed that life can only come from life. He demonstrated the first scientific evidence that living things are not produced from nonliving matter. Life arises only from preexisting life. All living things come into existence from one or more parents. If life can only come from life, then where did the first life come from? This leads to the conclusion that God created the first form of life in the very beginning. As in Genesis 1, God created every living thing after its kind. Various life forms were created by God separately after their kinds.

In order to explain the supposed origin of the long necked giraffe, evolutionists once believed "the use and disuse" theory.[5] According to both Darwin and Lamarck, giraffes started to stretch their necks to reach and eat green leaves in tall trees on the dried up African prairie. As a result, they developed long necks because their ancestors stretched for leaves in trees, then passed this trait to their offspring. But, traits acquired by use and disuse don't affect heredity. The use-disuse theory doesn't work and has been discarded. For example, will your newly born children be stronger if you use your muscles and get strong? Will your newly born children be smarter if you use and develop your brain? Even though you cut off the tails of mice for many generations, baby mice will still be born with tales.

Evolutionists say that evolution proceeded because of mutations and natural selection. According to the modern, neo-Darwinian theory, mutations are the source of new traits for evolution, and selection culls out the fittest combinations that are first produced by chance. Mutations are random changes by chance in the molecule of heredity, DNA genes. Mutations are real and certainly occur, but they occur very rarely, and most of them are harmful. Actually, mutations are blind, purposeless copying mistakes in the DNA. Also, natural selection does not produce new information, and it cannot select what has not been produced. Natural selection can only operate on the information already contained in genes. Therefore, mutation and natural selection cannot be the main causes for real evolution (macroevolution).

We have to distinguish between macroevolution and microevolution. Microevolution is "sub-speciation," which is the variation within the species, while macroevolution is "trans-speciation," which is the change from one type to others. It is true that the processes of mutation and natural selection produce microevolution (variation within type). But we have not observed the occurrence of macroevolution. Macroevolution requires the expansion of the gene pool and the addition of new genes to produce new species and new complex organs. In October of 1980, the world's leading evolutionists held a historic conference on "Macroevolution" in Chicago's Field Museum of Natural History to explain the presumed evolutionary change from simpler to more complex types (macroevolution). They concluded that one cannot logically extrapolate from mutation, selection, and sexual recombination to macroevolution (*Science*, Vol. 210, November 1980, pp 883-7).

Mendel's Hereditary Law states that a species cannot turn into another species. All life reproduces according to species and type. This law supports the Theory of Creation, which says that God created every living thing "after its kind," meaning every species was created individually. For example, many varieties of dogs can be produced, but never can we breed a dog from some other type of animal.

What about Fossil Records?

Fossils are hardened remains, or traces of life beings, preserved in the earth's crust. Many people believe that fossils are substantial evidence for proof of the Theory of Evolution. But is this really true? Let's find out.

If evolution is a true fact, there would be more than 1.5 million transitional forms linking each species since there are about 1.5 million species living on the earth. Therefore, one would expect numerous numbers of transitional forms of fossils.

However, there are no fossils showing gradual evolutionary progression throughout time. Let us examine one of the fossils that the evolutionists have suggested to be a typical link between species, the archaeopteryx. The archaeopteryx is supposedly the link between reptile and bird. It has claws on its wings and teeth in its mouth. But let us scrutinize the characteristics of some confirmed birds and reptiles. Claws are found on the ostrich, the touraco, and the hoatzin. The hoatzin itself has wrist bones, which should make it even more primitive than the archaeopteryx, yet the hoatzin is a confirmed bird. As far as reptiles and teeth are concerned, a common reptile such as the turtle has no teeth. The only conclusion that can be made about the archaeopteryx is that it is a rare bird.

Every major invertebrate type (clams, snails, jellyfish, worms, sponges, etc.) abruptly appears fully-formed, and every major type of fish known (supposedly the first vertebrate) abruptly appears fully-formed without a trace of ancestors or intermediate forms. No evolutionary transitional forms have ever been found anywhere on the earth. In fossil records, "missing links" are the rule. The fossil record gives excellent support for the Creation model.[6,7,8,9,23]

In the Theory of Evolution, it is said that the human race and the ape have a common ancestor. The so-called "ape-man," which is believed to be the life form between man and ape, is merely a figment of the imagination, collected and assembled from a very small number of rare remains. The skull of the Java Man, an example of one such "ape-man," was later reported to be the skull of the long arm gibbon, and the tooth of the Nebraska Man was eventually reported to be the tooth of an extinct pig.[6]

When God created man, He breathed His spirit through man's nostrils. Thus, unlike animals, the human being has his/her own spirit and strives to find and worship God. Each human is a spiritual creature, created not only for a time, but also for eternity. Humans were created not only for this world, but also for God. God loves us and wants to have a relationship with us. In the beginning, God created the heavens and the earth, and every living being "after its kind." And God created man in His own image.

Mathematical Probability Says "No" to Evolutionism

The logic of science is based on mathematics. Is it probable by mathematical probability that life is formed by time and chance? The cell is the basic structure which makes up every living thing, and it is basically made up of protein and DNA. Suppose that there are 100 amino acids. What would be the probability of forming a specific sequence of 100 amino acids for a protein? The probability is 10 to the 130th to 1 ($1/10^{130}$). This means that the probability is essentially zero. According to the scientist Dr. R. Kaplan, "If the chance for the formation of life was $1/10^{130}$, one could conclude that life could not have originated without a donor of life."[20] I also quoted the analogy made by Fred Hoyle, a British astronomer, who stated that the chance of forming a higher form of life out of the blue was comparable to the chance that "a tornado sweeping through a junkyard might assemble a Boeing 747 from the material therein."[22] A Boeing 747 plane is a collection of 4.5 million parts. No one will ever believe that a Boeing 747 can be built by a tornado sweeping through a junkyard. So how can one believe that life happened by chance? It is more plausible to believe that God designed and created life than to believe that life originated with a probability that is slim to none.

To demonstrate further on creationism, I discussed the core distinction between life and lifelessness. Consider a dead seed and a live seed. Both seeds possess the same organic structure and composition. However, if the dead seed is buried underneath the soil, it will decay and rot, and that will be the end of the story. On the contrary, if the live seed is buried underneath the same soil, it will produce little stems and leaves, and it will grow into a plant that will flower and bear fruit. That is a significant difference. In the living seed, there is a mysterious source of invisible energy or power that the dead seed does not possess. Life is not merely material, but rides upon matter. Life can be defined by what it does, not by what it is.

In a creationist's view, there is genetic information in DNA, and the formation of the information demands intelligence. Therefore, DNA was formed by intelligence. DNA is somewhat like a computer program on a floppy disk. Like a computer disk, DNA, itself, has no intelligence. The complex codes of DNA could only have originated outside of itself. The invisible source of life is given by the invisible Creator God.

Do you really think that the universe evolved by itself? The structure of a tiny leaf is much more complicated and sophisticated than most complicated modern scientific products, such as the space shuttle. God speaks to humans through the works of His hands. "Inside the human body, a simple form of protein can be produced in only 5 seconds, while outside the body, it would take 10^{50} years to produce the same kind of protein by chance."[21] The age of the earth itself is presumed to be around 4.5 billion (4.5 X 10^9) years, yet this is not enough time to produce a simple protein by chance, even though the human body can produce it instantly! Nothing exists without God, the Creator. Through His creations, He clearly shows His existence, wisdom, and power, but many people deny God's existence and walk aimlessly without Him.

One of the most debated topics these days concerns cloning. How should this be interpreted? Can this be regarded as creation of life? Recently, scientists have been able to develop the technology to clone a living life. One might think that this is a form of creating "life." However, these scientists are replicating a life from an already existing life (as the word "cloning" implies), rather than creating it, from scratch. Their beginning point originates from another "life." The cloning technology may have enabled one to "replicate" an already-living sheep, monkey, or dog, but no one has ever created the simplest form of life, such as living seeds, from organic chemicals. Life comes only from another living thing, not from a nonliving thing. There is a big chasm between a living and a nonliving thing. Although life resides in a body made of materials, the material is not life itself. The living life possesses a mysterious source of energy or power that transcends the realm of natural science.

Even though scientists will be able to encode the genetic information in synthesized organic compounds, they will not be able to create life itself. The biogenic principle says that life comes only from life. For me, it would take a much greater faith to believe in evolutionism than to believe in a Creator God.

Do Thermodynamic Laws Support Evolution?

The two Laws of Thermodynamics are known to be the most basic and universal laws of science. The First Law of Thermodynamics is known as the Law of Conservation of Energy (Mass). It states that the total amount of energy in the universe remains unchanged, and that energy can neither be created nor be destroyed. Then, where did the initial energy come from? The logical answer is to say that it must have been created by God from nothing to matter (energy).

The Second Law of Thermodynamics is also known as the Law of Increasing Entropy. (The word "entropy" from Greek is a measure of the degree of disorder in a structured system.) It states that as time elapses, everything runs down and tends toward the greatest state of randomness, thus, the highest entropy. This contradicts the Theory of Chemical Evolution, which assumes that inorganic substances organized themselves to produce complex life forms. Even in an open system, a preexistent mechanism is necessary for increasing the degree of order.[4]

I Am a Shouting Voice

The First International Conference on the Origin of Life in August 1980 was a huge success, having stirred up and challenged many participants. Five months later, on January 31, 1981, about 400 Christian scientists gathered to establish the Korea Association of Creation Science (KACS). They elected me as the first president of KACS.

Pastor Joon-Gon Kim, founder of Korean CCC, stated, "There are three major events in the history of Korean Christianity: The introduction of the Gospel into Korea through the American missionaries, Appenzeller and Underwood, in 1882; the complete translation of the Bible into the Korean language in 1948; and the foundation of KACS by Christian scientists rejecting evolutionism in 1981." As of 2005, KACS has approximately 2,000 members.

As I began my activities with KACS, criticism from evolution circles erupted. One newspaper article criticized me as a nonexpert who opposed the theory of evolutionism. My wife said to me, "Don't you think you should slow down a little until you produce some research results in Korea, so that they don't attack you as a pseudo-scientist?"

"This is a God-given opportunity, and if I don't shout it out, then God will use those stones outside to profess the truth of creation," I answered with determination.

My willingness to proclaim the truth about God brought me honor surpassing the criticism I was receiving at the time. Before long, I received news from the United States that I had been awarded the NASA Tech Brief Award of 1981, the result of a joint research project between NASA and the International Nickel Company (INCO) on super-heat-resistant alloys for aerospace applications. This was the second award for me, following the first award in 1976 from NASA. Soon thereafter, I also received the IR-100 Industrial Research Award from the United States.

While working as a professor at KAIST in 1983, I invented a new semiconductor lead-frame copper alloy (CDA-194) and obtained many international patents, which were used by Motorola in 1986. Because of my invention, I received the Korean President's Medal. I also received the King Sejong Award for contributions in science and technology. The success story of the Korean semiconductor material in the world markets captured society's attention and was broadcast as an industrial documentary on the national Korea Broadcasting System (KBS). In 1987, I was recognized as the "Scientist of the Year" by the Science Journalist Club of Korea. Domestic newspapers described me as "the goose that lays golden eggs." Consequently, many journalists who had been critical of me proclaiming creationism became supportive friends, and they reported many articles covering my research. I insisted that all awards and medals given to me were due to the almighty Lord enabling me to succeed. God placed medals on my shoulders and pushed me to courageously proclaim His creation and His power.

CHAPTER 3

How the Lord Is Using Me
for God's University

The Call to Lead God's University

*I*n February 1994 while I was a professor at the Korea Advanced Institute of Science and Technology (KAIST), I received a phone call inviting me to become the founding president of Handong, a new Christian university that was being established in Pohang, Korea. The name "Handong" is taken from *Han*, which means "Korea," and *Dong*, which is Chinese for "East." When I was first asked to take this position, my wife and I agonized over leaving KAIST, where I was enjoying the comfort of stability and a promising future. So after a few days, I kindly declined the offer. But the person called me again, suggesting that I might reconsider after visiting the university and seeking God's will in this matter. God reveals His will to us through prayer, words, and pastors' sermons.

After refusing the invitation, I had planned to travel to the United States to present a technical paper at a scientific conference. But for some unknown reason, my U.S. visa was delayed, and I could not leave the week I had planned on doing so. So I attended the Sunday worship service with my wife. Why, of all things, did a sermon entitled, "God's Calling and Obedience" from Genesis 12:1 happen on that particular Sunday? The pastor preached that when God orders us to leave, we should obey; otherwise, if we don't, we will encounter failures even if the conditions look favorable in the beginning. Inspired by a sermon about Abraham, who left his place of security in his homeland for an unknown land of promise, my wife and I decided to move by faith, trusting in the Lord.

I further received God's words and guidance in this matter through various pastors. Pastor J. Park preached at a prayer meeting in April 1994 that Handong was planned by God a long time ago to educate young people and to transform the world in the 21st century for Christ and His Kingdom. He foretold of difficulties and trials to Handong in the future similar to Nehemiah, who was faced with opposition in rebuilding the destroyed walls of Jerusalem (Nehemiah chapters 2 and 4). Also, in August 1996, God sent Pastor Jean Darnall of Youth with a Mission (YWAM) to Korea from Hawaii and had her pray for Handong. She also foretold of afflictions for Handong in the future, but she explained that the difficulties were necessary for Handong to become a true university for God's purposes. She compared the afflictions and difficulties of Handong with the heat required to cook a delicious soup. For that soup, all the ingredients in the cooking pot need to be boiled, because boiling produces the good taste.

God led me on path I could not see and by ways that I would never have chosen. When I faced desperate financial difficulties and trials, I prayed to the Lord and read the Bible, along with other Christian books on overcoming financial difficulties.[16-19] And I cried and sang my favorite hymns numerous times, including "Amazing Grace" and "Father, I Stretch My hands to Thee." One of the books I read that was especially relevant was *Rees Howells: Intercessor,* by Norman Grubb.[18] It intrigued me because of the similarities in God's guidance between the Bible College of Wales that opened in 1924 in England and Handong Global University that was established in 1994 in Korea. Both institutions were similar because both had a similar global vision. Mr. Rees Howells had been praying for the Gospel to spread to the world before he went over to Africa. When he returned home in 1920 after 6 years of missionary service from Africa, the Council of Mission appointed him a freelancer, to travel all over the English-speaking world as God led him to selected people everywhere.

But something unexpected was to happen to Mr. Rees Howells!! The Lord called him to start a new Bible college. God told him to build this college to train young people and to intercede for world evangelization. It came as a shock to him, and he asked for confirmation from God. Mr. Howells confirmed God's will through the Word in Chronicles 28:20, 21 *"Be strong and courageous and do the work. Do not be afraid or discouraged, for the Lord God, is with you. He will not fail you, nor forsake you, until all the work for the service of the temple of the Lord is finished."*

As Mr. and Mrs. Howells prayed over this, it tested their faith. It meant being called away from the very thing that most appealed to them — a worldwide revival ministry. It also meant new and large financial burdens in establishing a new college, for the Lord told them that they would have to do it by faith. On the other hand, all the finances for the worldwide ministry that he originally planned to participate in were provided by the Council of Ministry. The Council did not want to let Mr. Howells go. Finally, Mr. Howells and his wife gave themselves over to the Lord to be His instrument to build the Bible college. However, they had no idea how the finances would be supplied. Moreover, the year the college opened, 1924, was a time of great financial crisis in the world.

On the fifth anniversary of the Bible College of Wales in 1929, Mr. Howells published the first report. He said, "We want to give you a brief account of what has been accomplished during the last five years through faith and believing prayer. Thousands were watching the outcome of this venture of faith — a college without a committee, council, denomination or wealthy person behind it. During the last three years, it has been rare to have on hand sufficient funds to meet our necessities for three consecutive days. It has been the Father's will to teach us to trust Him each morning for the day's needs in order to give us a practical demonstration of His words: 'Give us this day our daily bread.' The Lord has been providing for us day by day and teaching us that living faith rises above our circumstances." The testimony of the Bible College of Wales by Rees Howells is almost the same as my testimony, which I experienced during the last ten years through Handong Global University.

Encountering Severe Financial Difficulty

The first unexpected and disastrous obstacle to Handong was the failure of the founder's business in 1994 before the university even opened. This was a great shock to all of us!! The ramifications of this financial downfall were serious. I was even tempted to return to KAIST because I was only on leave from there; but I could not go back. If the Almighty Creator God is leading Handong, why should I worry about its future? I had to pray to God and learn to trust Him. It is easier for one to say, "I trust God" when things are going smoothly. In this time of desperation, I meditated on the Scriptures. I read how Abram trusted God without knowing what the future held. In Genesis 12, the Lord called Abram and commanded him to go to the land that He would show him, promising that Abram would be a blessing. However, in the midst of this promise, there was a famine in the land (Genesis 12:10).

After Handong Global University opened, financial difficulties worsened due to the urgent need to construct additional dormitories and facilities. Every year, the Lord burdened me with the need to build more buildings and to provide accommodations for the increasing number of students. The university was still in debt for the newest dormitories, and I was, once again, facing the need for substantial loans. Even while I was still paying for the old dormitories and constantly looking to the Lord for the daily needs of the university, I had to move forward by faith and erect new buildings. Since tuition covered less than 70 percent of the school's operating expenses, Handong Global University experienced severe financial difficulties. For several months, the university could not even pay salaries for faculty, either in part or in whole. Sometimes, I lost sleep because I had to start a new construction without any money on hand. I wondered and asked God, "Why did You not give us enough funds to run Your university?"

I understood His will by reading Proverbs 30:7-9: "Two things I ask of you, Oh Lord! Do not refuse me before I die. Keep falsehood and lies far from me; give me neither poverty nor riches, but give me only my daily bread. Otherwise I may have too much and disown you and say, 'Who is the Lord?' Or I may become poor and steal, and so dishonor the name of my God." Agur, the writer of this proverb, did not ask God for wealth. He was afraid that if he were rich, he might feel self-sufficient and try to live without God. God uses troubles and weaknesses in our lives to teach us to rely on His mighty power.

Whether a dormitory, the chapel, or a classroom building, each of the buildings on Handong's campus is stained with tears that carry silent testimonies on how God used the

49

building when it was constructed to show that He is in control and that He is, indeed, the helping God. Truly, He is the living God who does not let the cries of His believers pass without His intervention. This was His way to show to the world with no uncertainty that Handong is His school that He founded for His Great Commission. For the task, He collected students from all over the world, future global leaders, who He wants to use for His purposes.

The Opening of Handong Global University

March 7, 1995 was the day when the first page of Handong's history book opened.

Handong opened in 1995, in Pohang, Korea, with 400 outstanding students, and in 2006, approximately 3,500 students from Korea and abroad enrolled, encompassing 58 nations

Students from all over the country came in waves, like young pioneers stepping onto the virgin soils of ancient lands. The campus was set in a wilderness of bitter ocean winds surrounded by hills and fields that had been frozen all winter long, but the school grounds, where the opening ceremony took place, were filled with warm sunlight. The faculty had worked through many nights preparing to receive the new family. The professors held early morning prayer meetings at the school prayer room and eagerly awaited their first contact with the students.

We celebrated three ceremonies that day: The opening of the school, the welcoming ceremony for the incoming students, and the inauguration of the school's first president. During Handong's inauguration ceremony of March 7, 1995, all Handong families, including the president, the professors, all staff, and the parents together with the students, entered the school in the wilderness, a school of suffering and prayers. Indeed, they were entering the school of the Holy Spirit, a blasting furnace in which raw ore would be refined into steel under intense heat and fire. During the process, all vain thoughts, worldly desires, and vanity would be burnt off and the residue would float as sludge. Only the refined, pure metal would be collected on the bottom as God's people.

Handong is, indeed, "God's small school" that produces a few broken people that God needs, like those featured in the book, *A Tale of Three Kings — A Study in Brokenness,* by Gene Edwards.[24] "God has a university. It's a small school. Few enroll; even fewer graduate. Very, very few indeed. God has this school because He does not have broken men and women. Instead, He has several other types of people. He has people who claim to have God's authority, and don't; people who claim to be broken, and aren't. And people who do have God's authority, but who are mad and unbroken. And He has, regretfully, a great mixture of everything in between. All of these He has in abundance, but broken men and women, hardly at all.

In God's sacred school of submission and brokenness, why are there so few students? Because all students in this school must suffer much pain. And as you might guess, it is often the unbroken ruler (whom God sovereignly picks) who metes out the pain. David was once a student in this school, and Saul was God's chosen way to crush David."

Imprisonment

Due to the university's financial hardship and because of the IMF (International Monetary Fund) turmoil in Korea in 1997, there was no money for the school to pay the professors' salaries. At that time, the Ministry of Education of the Korean government recognized Handong's achievement of academic reform for the 21st century, and the school received US$3 million in three years. Due to its financial deficiency, the university used the money to pay the professors' back salaries in December 1997, and reimbursed the funds according to their original designation the following month. This gave our local opponents a good excuse in the attempt to topple me from the position of Handong Global University's president. In May 2000, they accused the vice president of the university and me of misusing the government funds. The local court's verdict was guilty, and we were arrested at the courthouse and put into prison on May 11, 2001. The arrest of an active university president at court was a historically unprecedented event. On Teacher's Day, May 15, 2001, about 1,500 students, along with professors and 300 or so parents, gathered in front of the prison yard to comfort me in solidarity as I sat imprisoned. They sang my favorite hymn, "Amazing Grace."

Students and Parents at Prison Gate on Teacher's Day,
May 15, 2001

Through many dangers, toils, and snares
I have already come
This grace has brought me safe thus far
And grace will lead me home

They prayed for me and laid carnations down on my behalf. I was in prison for 53 days. I still remember the day when the jailors first handcuffed both my hands and tied my body with ropes to transport me to prison. As I was taken to the prison, my heart was crushed and I was in great distress. A sense of despair seeped into my heart.

I meditated on the humility and suffering of Jesus Christ. ***"Our Lord Jesus Christ, being in the very nature of God, did not consider equality with God something to be grasped, but emptied Himself as He took on the form of a servant and became like a human being. And being found in appearance as a man, He humbled himself and became obedient to death, even death on the cross" (Philippians 2:6-8).*** He was whipped and beaten for my sake. He bled on my behalf. He was sneered at and despised for my sake. But I was neither beaten nor thrashed. I was not ridiculed or dragged through the streets. Through my own suffering, however, trivial it might have been compared with what Jesus had to suffer, I thought I could appreciate, just a little, the shame and suffering that Jesus had experienced. What a spiritual blessing this was! As the days passed, I meditated on the humility of Jesus Christ. I began to pray to God to help me, and the Lord blessed me with His presence in the prison cell. It was so vivid that comfort from Him which filled my heart.

In prison, more than anything else, the thought of the suffering of Jesus overwhelmed me with a deeper understanding. Often, I shed tears because I knew that my pain and suffering were nothing compared to what my Lord Jesus had to bear on Calvary for me. No work of God can be accomplished unless it goes through the refining fire as no pure gold can result without going through a crucible fire. The Holy Spirit taught me to know that in God, an affliction can turn into a blessing despite the hardship it involves.

Thomas A. Kempis said, "There are many people who love Jesus so that they can go to heaven by believing in Christ and receiving salvation. But extremely few are those willing to carry Jesus' cross of suffering. Many people are happy to believe in Jesus and receive blessings. But very rare are those willing to taste suffering through sacrifice, loss, and pain for Jesus Christ's sake." Many say they love Jesus, but they love Him only when things are going well. Is our love for Jesus entangled with our own self-interests and convenience? Our spirit must be poor.

"Blessed are you who are poor, for yours is the kingdom of God" (Luke 6:20). We must not be proud or boastful, even if we have accomplished much. *"So you also, when you have done everything you were told to do, should say, 'We are unworthy servants; we have only done our duty'" (Luke 17:10).*

54

Diary in Prison

When the judge in the local court had finished reciting the verdict on May 11, 2001, and asked if I had anything to say, I was unable to answer for a while. I just stared blankly at him. My mind was stupefied, and I could not comprehend what the verdict meant. "Embezzlement," "Risk of tampering with the evidence," "Intentional avoidance of court appearance without just cause," "A possible escape overseas." Before I could think, the correctional officers came in and took me through the court's back doors. Once we stepped out through the doors, they put handcuffs on me. When I felt the cold handcuffs on my wrists, reality finally hit me.

While I was led to the prison, I closed my eyes and thought about what God's will might be through this unbelievable, helpless situation. The only thing that came into my mind was how shocked all my beloved family, students, professors, and students' parents would be. All of a sudden, I was at a complete loss. I did not even know what I was supposed to ask of God.

After being signed into the prison office, the other prisoners and I were led to the newcomers' admissions room. I took off all my clothes and put them in a sack, and I picked up a brown prison uniform from a pile in a corner under their orders. Because the pants that I had picked up were so big, I bent over to look for a smaller pair, but the guard said, "Just wear anything! They're all the same, so there's no point in choosing." I also put on the white rubber shoes placed in front of my feet.

"Take off your glasses! Prison rules do not allow metal-framed glasses. Tell your family to bring you plastic-rimmed glasses when they visit you."

I held up a board that said "Number 433" and was photographed standing in front of a wall, facing forward and sideways. It was the so-called mug shot for criminal records.

Wearing clothes that had belonged to a stranger, I didn't have any thoughts or feelings. After my glasses were confiscated, everything looked hazy. Holding a plastic spoon and two bowls that the guard had issued to me, I followed him to the cell to which I was assigned.

When I entered the cell, I saw the faces of those sitting inside as if I were in a thick fog. All their eyes were upon me. At that moment, someone said in a loud, angry voice, "Turn around and sit facing the wall!"

I did not know why, but I sat facing the wall for a long time. I found out later that it was part of being initiated into a room. After a long time, I heard the same voice again.

"Now turn around, and tell us your name, address, occupation, the nature of your crime, and your prior record — in the order as it reads on this piece of paper."

So I turned around, and after saying "hello" in a loud voice to everyone in the cell, I introduced myself according to the list, including the nature of my crime. As they were listening to my story, they began to comment, "That doesn't sound like something you should be arrested for. Something sounds wrong."

"They arrested an acting university president even before the final verdict had been reached? That seems unfair!"

Everyone had his own interpretation regarding my crime. Then, another voice said loudly, "That Handong Global University is a problematic school!"

They all seemed as knowledgeable about the law as any attorney did. Then, a man who appeared to be the leader in the cell asked, "President, have you had lunch?"

Only then did I realize that I had skipped lunch. It was already past 4 o'clock in the afternoon.

"Hey, give him that piece of bread!"

My wife asked me later, "Did you eat that bread? You were able to eat in that situation?"

"Of course; it was very good. I was hungry." I smiled. My wife did not know whether to smile or cry, wondering how I could have had the peace of mind to eat in such a situation.

My fellow cellmates were very considerate of me. There were two small tables in that room, and the cell leader allowed me to put my bowls on one of them. He also exempted me from clean-up duties. At 9 pm, it was time to sleep. I wondered how all these men could sleep in such a small room. Each person rolled his blanket into a pillow, and 35 men were arranged in order. Every other man lay down with his head facing the opposite way, and we were all lying on our sides so that our noses almost touched the feet of the men lying next to us. We were literally like sardines in a can.

"You may be No. 8! If you were to be placed according to when you were admitted here, you'd be last and sleeping next to the bucket (toilet bowl), so be grateful for your promotion."

Prison rules dictated that we sleep with the lights on. With such bright lights above us, everyone seemed to have a difficult time falling asleep. Perhaps out of boredom since everyone was lying down, yet awake, the room leader said, "Let's each talk about what we've been through in the outside world."

Everyone talked about how they had regretted their lives — how they shouldn't have done this or that. Finally, it came my turn.

"I don't have much to say, but could I sing instead? My hometown is in an isolated region, now submerged by the construction of a dam. So I'm a wanderer without a hometown, and I like this song called 'The Spring of My Hometown.'"

"You want to sing? Go ahead."

I began to sing in a low voice a song that I learned in elementary school like many others there.

*My hometown, a mountain village
with blooming flowers:
Peach, apricot, and baby azaleas ...*

Soon, all the others started to sing along with me. When I finished singing, someone said, "Hmm, President Kim, you sing pretty well." The atmosphere had changed. The song that most everybody learned in their elementary schools became the bond of friendship with my cellmates on that first night in prison. Even they seemed to briefly forget their depression and the fact that they were in confinement. I closed my eyes and thought about the mountains of my hometown. All of a sudden, sorrow burst inside my heart and I could not hold back my crying as I thought, *I'm now 62 years old. How can I be in this kind of place, lying like this now? They say that the nature of my crime is "evil," and there is a risk that I may flee overseas? That I intentionally avoided court appearances?* But having broken the literal letter of the law and awaiting the final verdict, I reflected upon myself and my past.

We lay next to each other, our clothes and our flesh almost touching, with our breath so close to each other's that we couldn't tell whether it was ours or someone else's. Lying down in that cell filled with 35 men placed side by side, I stood before God as a bare, naked soul.

For My Thoughts Are Not Your Thoughts

Honestly, I didn't know what to think for a couple of days. I was in a prison that I hadn't even imagined in my wildest dreams. I believed that *"In all things God works for the good of those who love him" (Romans 8:28)*, but I meditated yet again on God's will that had brought the vice president and me to this prison after all that had happened.

"For my thoughts are not your thoughts, neither are your ways my ways, declares the Lord. As the heavens are higher than the earth, so are my ways higher than your ways and my thoughts than your thoughts" (Isaiah 55:8-9).
I realized that a prison, too, was a world of its own with real people living in it, and that it was a bearable place. Each person in that place was born with a precious life, and each person's life had its own circumstances, tears, sighs, and sorrows that only that individual could tell. Each man was searching for his own hope.

Three days into my imprisonment, on the morning of Teachers' Day, the guard asked me discreetly, "President Kim, haven't you heard any news?"

"How can I hear any outside news when I'm sitting here inside the high prison walls?" I answered.

"Thousands of Handong students are coming here in honor of Teachers' Day. The prison officers are preparing for an emergency, and everyone seems nervous. I'm a little worried, too."

"I'm sure nothing will happen. Our students are mature and wise," I answered.

That afternoon, the prison officer came to me with a bright face.

"President Kim, you've really educated your students well. They finished their procession in complete order, and when they left, there wasn't a single speck of trash left behind. What would we have to worry about if all our citizens' demonstrations were like that? I've never been so moved in my 20 years as a prison guard."

I cannot tell you how proud I was of our students at that moment. After a week of imprisonment, I was moved to a cell with only seven people. Everyone in that cell was a newcomer, so I didn't have to go through another initiation. Only then was I able to focus on each person in my cell. I wrote out the Lord's Prayer and the Apostle's Creed for each person, and I suggested that we give thanks to God for each meal. Strangely, no one objected.

I prayed whenever someone had to appear in court. In this way, I was able to calm my heart and share God's grace with my cellmates each day. For seven years, I hadn't had a day of rest, free from worrying about money. It was nice to be able to meditate on the Bible without worrying about money after such a long time. I read all the books that I hadn't been able to read before, and I had nothing to do except to pray and sing praises while I was in prison. I began to think that perhaps God was giving me a special vacation since I had been so busy up to that point. In that place, I prayed the prayer of Jabez for Handong every day.

"Oh, that you would bless me (Handong) and enlarge my (Handong's) territory! Let your hand be with me (Handong) and keep me (Handong) from harm so that I (Handong) will be free from pain" (I Chronicles 4:10).

Later on, I wrote down my confession in my notebook. "My spirit stands before God, shaking. I have never stood before Him like this, with absolutely nothing such as my name, honor, position, pride, pains, and anxiety. I am living the true freedom of having shed all those things. I have been running with my focus only on what is ahead, and God has now allowed me to stop for a while, and in this strange place, through this strange method, He has freed me and is meeting with me, one-on-one. This is my place of prayer, my attic where I meet with the Lord."

Cellmates in the Prison

Eighteen days into my imprisonment at Kyoungju Prison, on May 28, the warden came to me and said in a low voice, "You'll be moved to Daegu Prison in preparation for the Appellate Court trials there. Don't tell anyone, but get ready by 10 o'clock tomorrow morning."

When I thought about leaving the next day, my heart was in turmoil over my cellmates. I realized what it meant to live together day in and day out in the same room, breathing the same air. In the morning of my departure, I desperately prayed for each person in my room. I began to cry.

"Father God, thank You for allowing us to meet here. We are in a tough place, but even a prison becomes a place of peace and thanks because You are here with us. Have mercy on these men and bless them so they may become Your children. Let them become bearers of the evidence that You are with us on this earth. Watch over them as the apple of Your eye. Protect their families. No matter how long they may have to stay in here, let them learn of a new life through patience, and let their days become days of growth of their faith."

We all said our good-byes in tears. When I came outside with my sack, all the prisoners who were to be transferred to Daegu Prison were lined up and roped, like a string of dead fish. My hands were cuffed and a thick rope bound me from shoulder to waist, front and back. I could hardly move because the handcuffs were so tight on my wrists, and I couldn't even lean back on my chair because of the thick rope across my back.

Then, the warden came to me and said, "President Kim, please understand. This is the rule. After an escape incident recently, our rules require us to put two handcuffs on each person."

I recalled a letter that one of my old cellmates there sent to Handong after he was released while I was still in prison:

Hello! I spent a month with President Kim in May 2001 while he was at Kyoungju Prison. I'd like to tell you about the man whom I saw and experienced firsthand.

61

The month that I spent with President Kim was a truly precious period of time for me. He always started and ended each day in prayer. He seemed more like some nice man living next door than a university president. After watching him never losing his smile and always living in prayer even during his difficult times in prison, I, too, repented of my own life. He stayed up late into the night reading all the countless letters that the school sent him every day, reading every word on each page.

I still remember that day. The morning of the day that he was to be transferred to Daegu Prison, he knelt down and prayed with tears of sorrow. He prayed for Handong rather than for himself, and he cried as he prayed for all his students. I do not know all the details of the incident, but I thought it incredible that a man like him showed no resentment toward anyone.

To everyone at Handong, I ask that you write many letters of encouragement to President Kim and send him hope. I think all of you are lucky to be attending Handong, where President Kim is the captain."

He Lowered Himself

The bus left Kyoungju Prison and drove toward Daegu Prison on Highway 1. The mountains and fields were covered with lush summer green. The outside scenery was very familiar, and yet, everything seemed new. I had a million emotions surging within me, and I began to weep. I, too, felt scorned and wronged, but it was not because of my sorrow that I cried. After being handcuffed and roped, the weight of the pain that our Lord must have had to endure was heavy upon me. His crown of thorns, the whips, the spits, the insults! His loneliness and sorrows, the shame and betrayal — I thought I could feel all those emotions piercing my heart. Jesus Christ, who is God the Creator, came to this world as a man, and that is the culmination of humility and lowering of oneself.

"Your attitude should be the same as that of Christ Jesus: Who, being in very nature God, did not consider equality with God something to be grasped, but made himself nothing, taking the very nature of a servant, being made in human likeness. And being found in appearance as a man, he humbled himself and became obedient to death — even death on a cross!" (Philippians 2:5-8).

When I thought about how much Jesus had to lower himself, I felt everything that I was going through was nothing in comparison. God had to take a human form in order to save me, a sinner — it was the only way for forgiveness! I could feel throughout my heart and body the love of God who sent His only son to die for me because nothing could be accomplished without the price of such a sacrifice. Jesus obeyed all the way to His death, and He became my way, my truth, and my life!

"For even the Son of Man did not come to be served, but to serve, and to give his life as a ransom for many" (Mark 10:45).

I am a being who has received such love and sacrifice! But I, the true sinner, am traveling so comfortably on a bus! While thinking of God's love, I cried because I was so thankful, and I cried because I felt so sorry.

When we arrived at Daegu Prison, Vice President Oh was grouped with the "pending" prisoners, and I was sent to a "convicted" prisoner's single cell room. As I passed the prison office, some of the prison guards who had been reading the newspaper looked up and recognized me.

"President Young-Gil Kim of Handong Global University, you are the elder who was the chairman of the Korea

Association for Creation Research, right? We were just reading about you in newspapers."

They were members of a Christian group in prison. They commented on how strange it was that the school itself had not said anything against its president, even if its faculty and staff would have been the first to know if the president had truly done anything wrong.

About a month after my transfer to Daegu Prison, Christian guards came to me and said, "We think that you are going to leave this place soon, and so we prepared a special event tonight. Please join us and share your testimony with us."

And so in the Christian gathering, I preached on Philippians 2:5-11. After the ceremony, they put their hands on my shoulders and prayed for me.

"We, the Church of Smyrna in this prison, send you, Elder Young-Gil Kim, as a missionary to the outside world."

Their tears fell on my shoulders and hands.

"President Kim, when you are released into the outside world, please don't forget about us, the Church of Smyrna."

I still remind myself, "I'm a missionary sent by the Church of Smyrna."

For Surely I Will Deliver You

December 28, 2001 was the day that I will never forget as long as I live. The appeal trial at the Daegu Appellate Court was to open at 10 o'clock in the morning. The trial that had begun in early spring continued through the dead heat of summer and was finally to end in the winter with a final verdict, and December 28 was the day. There had been a total of five of such sessions including the final one, each, of which, I was required to be present in person since the case was a criminal case. But this was the session where the final verdict was to be delivered that would determine my presidency of Handong Global University.

The Appellate Court verdict was crucial for me since its ruling would be essentially the final verdict for me for all practical purposes. In Korea, the Supreme Court is the highest court and is higher than the Appellate Court; however, it rarely overturns a verdict by the Appellate Court. That verdict could mean that I would be discharged from my position as the president of Handong, and then, I would not know what the fate would be of the school known as God's school.

The night before the final court appearance, I prayed to God as Jesus prayed on the mount of Gethsemane the night before he was to die on the cross, "Oh, Lord, please hold me tight so that my faith in You may not be weakened, the faith that declared that You would be on my side. Please allow me to be acquitted if it is truly Your will that I lead Your school."

Many Handong parents, students, and professors as well as the local media had already gathered outside the court to hear the final verdict and were waiting for the court session to begin. Everyone looked anxious, wondering what the final verdict would be. It was a sunny day, but a gusty, chilly, December wind was blowing through the court grounds, kicking up dust as if wanting to sweep away all our past trials and hardships.

Some passing people outside the court building were wondering what was happening in the courthouse that morning and asked, "Is there anything important going on in the courthouse today?"

I hurriedly headed to Courtroom 41, leaving behind many inquisitive faces as I had done numerous other times prior to that. A multitude of professors and parents numbering several hundreds were all headed toward the courtroom with me.

I was led to a seat in front with the vice president, along with other prisoners who came for other cases. The court was jam-packed. As the time approached the appointed hour to begin, it became dead silent inside. You could hear a pin drop. The few minutes that we waited for the judges to appear seemed like hours. Finally, we were all told to rise and the judges entered the room, as usual. They directly headed up to the podium and handled other, less significant cases first. Finally when our case number was called, the presiding judge went up to the podium and took about ten minutes to read the verdict. While the verdict was being read, my thoughts wandered around from the incident of the first phone call inviting me to become the founding president of the school through the sermon on Sunday when my trip to the U.S. was postponed.

In the end, the chief judge declared solemnly that the accused was NOT GUILTY of the major offenses stemming from the false accusation.

Then all of a sudden, the people in the courtroom all sprung up and approached me. Immediately, I was surrounded by people who shook my hand and hugged me.

Tears flowed endlessly on my cheeks, and I thanked God. Many others who came for my support were also weeping. "Father God, You, again, showed me that You are on our side and truly did assign me this job, and You have taken the burden from me!"

I felt so unreal. How long have I been waiting for this moment? How many years have I suffered, and how many sleepless nights have I knelt down and prayed to God in desperation? How many of our professors, parents, students, and other supporters prayed for this day? This was a victory for all the Handong family, and it was brought about by the hand of God.

I thought about Jesus who was resurrected from the dead. I thought this was a glimpse of how Jesus must have felt when He was raised from the tomb on the third day after He died on the cross and was entombed.

By the time I left the courthouse, the people outside waiting for the verdict had already heard the news. They were unable to hide their joy. The media all reported on the verdict: "After numerous trials and controversy, the current president and vice president of Handong are now acquitted on most of the accounts. After the first trial, the lower court had found them guilty on all accounts and the men had been arrested in court, but later they were released on bail. But the Appellate Court overturned the earlier verdict from the lower court." The eyes and ears of the country had been glued to the appeal, and the Appellate Court overturning the lower court's decisions again drew great interest across the country.

During an interview, the chairman of the Parents' Association said, "I'm overjoyed. We all prayed that we would get a verdict that would not interfere with President Kim doing his job. God has answered our prayers."

Attorney Lee told us that this verdict was a 120 percent victory for the school. God caused us to pray up to the very last minute so that we may not become proud of ourselves! It was a dramatic reversal by God. *"In the Lord I take refuge. How then can you say to me: 'Flee like a bird to your mountain. For look, the wicked bend their bows; they set their arrows against the string to shoot from the shadows at the upright in heart. When the foundations are being destroyed, what can the righteous do?' The Lord is in his holy temple; the Lord is on his heavenly throne. He observes the sons of men; his eyes examine them"* (Psalm 11:1-4).

Opposition with Miracles

Another problem that we faced was that some of the local people were strongly opposed to the establishment of a genuine Christian university in the city of Pohang. These people insisted that Handong Global University be converted into a public city university instead of keeping it as a private, Christian university. Finally, they initiated a petition drive in the streets and among the individual houses of Pohang. Those who opposed us obtained approximately 100,000 signatures in support of the conversion of Handong University into a city university. Their argument was that although Handong University was founded in Pohang, the citizens of Pohang did not receive any benefits from it. They argued that since Handong had always attracted students with only outstanding grades in and out of the country, many Pohang area students could not qualify for admission. They wanted to convert Handong into a school where any student from the Pohang area could be admitted without difficulty. As the president of the university, I could not accept that request from the citizens of Pohang, and therefore, I declined their recommendation.

Furthermore, they submitted to the Ministry of Education a 5,000-page petition, with 20 signatures per page, to transform Handong into a public university. The Ministry of Education sent 10 of these pages to Handong University as proof that they had received around 100,000 signatures from the local community. The Handong community felt very cornered, as if there were no way out. If the Ministry of Education honored this petition, Handong would face a very difficult challenge indeed.

However, again a miracle happened. We discovered that one page of the petition contained a signature stamp of a Handong faculty member. When the school showed that page to this faculty member for verification, he was startled because he had neither seen it before nor had he signed it! The faculty member whose name was found on that particular page testified that he never signed the petition. Apparently, someone had forged his signature stamp. As a result, we were able to prove that one of the pages that the Ministry of Education had sent to us contained a forged

68

signature, which discounted the credibility of the entire petition. As a result, the entire signed petition of all 5,000 pages was invalidated by the Ministry of Education. The probability of picking that one particular page in a lottery would be 1 in 5,000. A miracle indeed!! This is just one of the many miracles that God has performed for Handong.

Local people filed numerous lawsuits against the school and against me. I was indicted and had to appear in court so many times. But God intervened in each one of the lawsuits, and the school won every case.

Since opening in 1995, Handong, under God's providence, has accomplished uncommon growth and achievements. God called the first 400 students to the school in 1995. There are now about 135 full-time faculty members and 3,500 students from both Korea and abroad, about 90 percent of whom live in on-campus dormitories. There are ten schools in the undergraduate program of studies, and there are ten majors in the graduate programs, of which international law, global management, and information technology are offered entirely in English.

Handong was quoted by a major Korean daily newspaper as a "small but great school" and is called a model university for 21st century education because it is pioneering and developing an innovative education curriculum. Handong has won outstanding awards for educational reform for the 21st century from the Korean Ministry of Education several times. Students are chosen from among the top 7 percent of high school students in Korea. They have won numerous awards and honors from national and international competitions during and after their education.

The historical first commencement was held on Feb. 24, 1999, as a worship service full of thanks and grateful tears.

Handong's First Historic Commencement on Feb. 24, 1999

These Handong graduates, called "History Makers," were employed by world-class, multinational companies. Handong people pray that Handong graduates will guide key national institutions and fields in the area of business, media, diplomacy, courts, education, technology, government, and Christian religion.

Handong People as a 21st Century Nehemiah

Handong educates global Christian leaders in the 21st century just as the great, godly Nehemiah did in his generation in 450 B.C. Nehemiah was one of the most inspiring leaders in the Bible. God chose him to rebuild the destroyed walls of Jerusalem, and I always wondered why God chose him for that purpose. Nehemiah was neither an architect nor an engineer, but a cupbearer in the king's palace in Persia. From a worldly point of view, God should have selected a person with experience, knowledge, or management skills to rebuild the destroyed wall. But He chose Nehemiah because he was honest and trustworthy. Otherwise, the Persian king would not have selected him as part of his security staff, especially considering that he was a foreigner.

Nehemiah faced opposition from the outside and financial difficulties from within. When his people became discouraged and tired, he prayed and directed their vision toward God. He endured insults, intimidation, and treachery, walking through them with his head high and his eyes wide open, and with much prayer. Nehemiah had the faith to believe and to proclaim, "The God of Heaven will give us success." He was used by God to achieve the spectacular work of rebuilding and completing the wall in the amazingly short time of only 52 days, after it had been left in disrepair for as long as 150 years. *"When all our enemies heard about this, all the surrounding nations were afraid and lost their self-confidence, because they realized that this work had been done with the help of our God" (Nehemiah 6:16).* Nehemiah accomplished the seemingly impossible task because of his complete dependence upon God.

As the foremost Christian university in Asia, Handong began realizing its dream of cultivating servant leaders who will change the world. Given Korea's competitive advantages in geographic location and cultural affinity, Handong places its focus on serving and changing those developing countries in Asia. Handong will serve as the springboard into the unreached nations in Asia by spurring their economic development through the higher education of future leaders.

When I look back at Handong's living history covering the past ten years, I cannot but confess that everything concerning Handong is nothing but GOD'S PLAN being realized for His purpose in the 21st century. It is not a plan devised or choreographed by anybody, certainly not by the president of the school, the chairman, or anybody else. Everything took place the way it did according to God's providence. Students' tuition covers about 70 percent of the school's budget, and the rest of the budget is supported by the grass-roots supporters, named the "Papyrus Basket."

I believe that Handong's history is not a miracle. Rather, it is nothing other than the pilgrim's progress of the university, the realization of God's plan, which is intended to show us that Handong is God's school and He is the Living God working day and night for us down to seemingly trivial details, reaching even to remote corners of the world. Clearly, the Lord showed us that it is still possible that an institution can be established using God's principles, starting from nothing in a wilderness and coming to fruition in only a very short period of time. It is possible even in this modern time, which is full of secular ideas and respect only for materialistic accomplishments, a time when voices of despair and doomsday scenarios are rampant.

Even if the founder's business encountered calamity before the university's opening, leaving its future totally unknown, students came in droves, and not just ordinary students. These were students who mostly turned down opportunities to study in "Korean Ivy League schools," with a guaranteed future. They did so willingly because this unknown entity was founded purely on Christian principles. How thirsty and desperate they must have been!

Handong's history is filled with tears from the trials and hardships we have encountered and joy from triumph and victory after enduring them. The endless lawsuits and criminal litigations against the chartered president were originated by people whom God mobilized — even as He mobilized Babylonians to train Jews in the Bible. So they trained and forged the president, the faculty, and the students for the arduous tasks ahead of them. Through these people and what they did, everything has worked together to show the world that Handong is, indeed, *God's* school, which God is taking care of and guiding.

In Handong's short existence, Handong graduates have already spread all over the world, carrying out God's mission as they were taught. Some are in remote areas of the world, helping countries in need; others are in some of the world's most renowned institutions, such as Harvard, Yale, and Columbia, pursuing further education; still others are in high government positions in third-world countries, making important decisions for those countries. Handong opened the first American-style law school in Asia, Handong International Law School (HILS), in 2002, and so far, 15 students have passed the U.S. Bars. In 2006, the Ministry of Education of the Korean Government has selected Handong as a New University of Regional Innovation(NURI) for educating global leaders.

The Birth of the Papyrus Basket

At the time of Moses' birth in the Old Testament, all the Hebrew male babies born in Egypt were ordered to be killed. Moses' fate was like a lit candle in a storm. His parents made a bold decision. They recognized that they could no longer raise their child in hiding. They now had to send him down the river, entrusting his life in God's hands. They must have mourned and wailed as they weaved the papyrus basket in which they would lay their baby. But God moved on human hearts, and He miraculously saved the life of baby Moses through the hands of an Egyptian princess, the very daughter of the king who attempted to kill all Hebrew male babies. The papyrus basket, thus, played a crucial role in rescuing Moses, who later became the leader of the Israelites. *"She became pregnant and gave birth to a son. When she saw that he was a fine child, she hid him for three months. But when she could hide him no longer, she got a papyrus basket for him and coated it with tar and pitch. Then she placed the child in it and put it among the reeds along the bank of the Nile. His sister stood at a distance to see what would happen to him" (Exodus 2:2-4).*

Handong had undergone gut-wrenching birth pains and frightening persecution that exceeded what we could imagine. No longer were we able to hide our poverty amidst the escalating financial crises, so Handong decided to weave its own basket. A professor from KAIST suggested a fund-raising drive of $1 or $10 per account, in which anyone could participate. A few professors named the fundraising drive the "Papyrus Basket." Each individual strand of papyrus was weak by itself, yet countless strands came together to form the life-saving basket that saved Moses' life. Likewise, a donation of $1 or $10 per month was like a single strand of papyrus. However, the papyrus basket woven with the prayers of our supporters would become the tar and pitch that would protect Handong against secularization.

As the papyrus basket housed Moses, who was later used as God's man to save His chosen race, Handong Global University is like the papyrus basket that would house God's children, who would grow to be used by God to save all nations. The papyrus basket contained our desperate faith, that Handong is God's school and He is on our side and guides us for protection.

In February of 1998, not long after the Papyrus Basket was launched in Korea, the Handong International Foundation (HIF) was born at the Cornerstone Church, located at 24428 S. Vermont Avenue, Harbor City, California 90710, as a nonprofit, tax-exempt organization. Their e-mail address is:lahandong@hotmail.com; telephone (310) 530-4040. Shortly afterwards, other HIF chapters were established in Washington, D.C., and Seattle, Washington.

CHAPTER **4**

Why Not Change the World?

New Educational Paradigm for the New Era

*H*istorically, we have changed from a hunter-and-gatherer's economy to an agrarian economy and then to an industrial economy. The industrial economy gave way to the information economy, where we are at now. We will move into biotechnology and bio-economy in the not too distant future. During the next couple of decades, the info-technology and biotechnology ages may overlap. The bridge between computer code and genetic code may lead to a blurred demarcation between inorganic and organic life forms.[25] In the future bio-economy, economic value may be created at the molecular level, which is now called nanotechnology. The globalization and quickly changing technologies also blur the demarcation of traditionally dissimilar disciplines.

The most important economic development in recent years has been the rise of a new system for creating wealth, based no longer on muscle and machine, but on mind and knowledge. Labor in the advanced economy no longer consists of working on "things," but instead, it involves people acting on information and information acting on people. In the information age of the present century, the real power of a nation is determined by its knowledge capacity, which is the amount of knowledge that its people possess, i.e., knowledge, creativity, ingenuity, and wisdom. The yardstick for measuring the knowledge capability of a nation within the information-based society is the educational level of its people, upon which its economic and social development is based. Due to the direct dependency of a nation's power on this educational level in contemporary information societies, the importance of education cannot be overemphasized.

The new age demands a new paradigm of higher education. The educational paradigm of the 21st century will be far different from that of the 20th century, which was successful.[26] As Lew Platt, former CEO of Hewlett Packard succinctly states, "Yesterday's recipe for success clearly will not be tomorrow's recipe for success."

Each era produces its problems as well as its own benefits, with the problems getting progressively more serious as we march into successive eras. As this occurs, a greater need for education is felt, carrying progressively higher dimensions of significance. The industrial age was accompanied by pollution and environmental degradation that started out as local, national, and then global issues. The major problem in this information era is privacy and the enormous power of the technology that can cause a major global disruption in international commerce by unleashing its catastrophic consequences if used wrongly. In the bio-economy era in the future, the issue may even be greater; i.e., ethics with its potential impact on the very existence of the human being and all living species on earth, with consequences in epic proportions. The only way to address and alleviate these problems is comprehensive higher education for future global leaders addressing not only the academic elements, but also all human, moral, and spiritual aspects with an overall global perspective.

The middle of the 1990s was the epoch-making years for entering into the information technology-driven global community. The commercial use of the World Wide Web (www) began in 1994. Then GATT (General Agreement on Tariffs and Trade) was changed to the WTO (World Trade Organization), which gave impetus to the global economy. The establishment and opening of Handong Global University in 1995 coincides with the opening of the 21st century IT-driven global community.

Global Vision and Educational Philosophy of Handong

When Handong Global University planned to open in 1995, there were already a total of 159 universities in Korea. I asked myself, "Why do we need one more university?" The reason is because when Handong's graduates go into the world in the 21st century, they will face a totally different world, a global, technology-driven world. So Handong must educate its students by employing a new educational curricula needed for the 21st century global community. Our current universities are in dire need of a paradigm shift, calling for a revolutionary and fresh approach. Handong's purpose is to prepare our young students to live and work in an increasingly complex and challenging dynamic world.

True education is not simply conveying and transmitting knowledge, but cultivating the moral and spiritual realms as well. The whole person, or holistic education of academics, character, and faith with a global perspective is the cornerstone for Handong Global University. We recognize that it is essential to educate the whole person — academically, morally, and spiritually — in this century's high-speed digital global world. Handong's holistic educational framework for the 21st century can be depicted using the Chinese character for engineering.

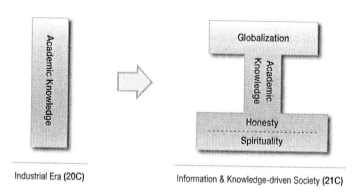

Industrial Era (20C)

Information & Knowledge-driven Society (21C)

The Shift and Change of the Educational Paradigm
from the 20th to the 21st century

The base foundation in the railway-type structure corresponds to moral and spiritual education, while the vertical component of the structure indicates knowledge or education. The upper bar points to globalization. The stability of the entire structure largely depends on the stability and strength of its foundation and the "I," or vertical beam. Therefore, knowledge accumulation without moral and spiritual foundation may result in weakening or collapse. The eventual use of knowledge is to help others. Education is not just for self-fulfillment or career enhancement. Christian education has a higher purpose, to be used for the Kingdom of God. Christian higher education can be a powerful tool for the restoration of the fallen world into the Kingdom of God.[28]

The very foundation of Handong's education is based on the faith of the Creator God. *"For from him and through him and to him are all things. To him be the glory forever! Amen"(Romans 11:36).* Character education is built upon faith education. The most important character education at Handong is honesty and integrity. The main purpose of

Handong is to educate honest and competent global Christian leaders for changing the world.

The people of Handong proclaim their vision with the motto, **"Why Not Change the World?"** It may seem bold or even unrealistic for a young university to embrace such a sweeping vision. Yet, we are convinced that this is our calling from God. Handong's God-given slogan is its people's dream and aspiration, for it is a signal call for Handong graduates to change the world through the power of the Holy Spirit. Our Lord Jesus Christ said, *"Do not conform any longer to the pattern of this world, but be transformed by the renewing of your mind. Then you will be able to test and approve what God's will is — his good, pleasing, and perfect will"* *(Romans 12:2).*

The university's vision below represents Handong's dream and aspiration; it is a long-term goal of where Handong is going:

> Handong Global University will be a Christian leadership university, educating 21st century leaders for Korea and the world, men and women who embody academic excellence, Christian moral character (in **particular, honesty and integrity**), **and global leadership.**

Handong seeks to prepare individuals who will become global leaders in their chosen professions in this globalized, technology-driven information age. The university is fully committed to achieve this vision through innovative, pragmatic, academic programs, and by providing a Christian community where students and faculty learn and practice a life integrating faith and learning.

Below are the mission statements outlining the set of actions the university will undertake to achieve its vision.

Handong will educate and cultivate 21st century leaders who are:

- **Honest Christian laymen,** who will change the world through a spirit of love, humility, and service for the glory of God;
- **Honest global servants,** who will serve communities, nations, and the world, especially developing countries, through their professionalism and ethics;
- **Honest intellectuals** in various academic fields, who, with a Christian worldview, will reestablish the true purpose of education and restore Biblical creationism and impaired morality.

As a Christian educator and as the administrator of Christian higher education, I have long struggled to formulate an ideal model of Christian higher education. For I am absolutely convinced that Handong Global University, as God's university, has a special mission granted by the Creator God. I believe that the ideal Christian higher education of today must be distinguished from secular higher education in terms of its institutional contexts and its educational approaches.

Handong Education Development Center (HEDC) has, thus, assisted me in developing a practical paradigm for "The Handong B.E.S.T. Mission" that will be fulfilled via 4C-Approaches (COMMITMENT, COMPETENCE, COMPASSION, and CONVERSION) and 2C-Contexts (CREATOR and COMMUNITY). This diagram has been constructed to visualize the 4 Cs around Faith, which represents the essential components of Handong's Christian higher education: Biblically-Based COMMITMENT, Education-Centered COMPETENCE, Stewardship-Oriented COMPASSION, Transformation-Aimed CONVERSION = B.E.S.T.

◦ The **B.E.S.T.** Global Handong 2010

Handong B.E.S.T. Mission

The invisible hand of God will be made visible through Handong. The world in His hand is the Global Community, to which Handong graduates are sent upon His calling. Handong's educational foundation is Faith in the Lord, the CREATOR, and its Mission Field is the Global COMMUNITY. As President of Handong Global University, I rejoice in the Lord God because of His special calling for Handong to carry out the "B.E.S.T. Mission" in this globalized world today. I have committed myself to serve Him by getting this mission accomplished.

God has been transforming Handong into a genuine God's university with clear global vision and mission. Handong cannot be all things to all countries. It's educational strategy for global mission is to bring in and educate promising young men and women from the developing nations. The educational curriculum at Handong accents practical knowledge and skills needed for nation building and economic development with moral and spiritual reflection. Handong focuses on educating international students, especially from developing countries in the world. These students receive high technology educational opportunities, not otherwise provided in their home countries. These international students not only receive excellent academic training for economic development and global awareness, but they also receive moral and spiritual training as well. It is Handong's ultimate goal to send those students back as future leaders to change and develop their nations as indigenous Christian leaders.

From its opening in 1995, HGU developed a new educational curriculum according to the demands of industry. Handong's education has been both demand-driven and purpose-driven from its beginning, and has shifted towards globalization and the digital world. Global leadership requires both ability and character. Multidisciplinary knowledge is essential for competent global leadership. Handong requires all students to study English and Chinese for global communication ability and also requires students to be familiar with computer platforms. Everyone is required to take double majors in allied fields in order to cultivate problem-solving abilities. Since its opening in 1995, HGU conducts all exams without monitors under the "Handong Honor Code."

Handong is a member university of the Global Engineering Education Exchange (GEEE) Program, administered by the International Institute of Education, New York. GEEE members comprise 46 universities in the USA, Europe, and Asia. Handong also has a partnership with World Vision and UNESCO for educating future leaders of developing countries such as Afghanistan, Mongolia, and Uzbekistan, as well as other countries.

"Peace and prosperity in the 21ˢᵗ century depend on increasing the capacity of people to think and work on a global and intercultural basis. As technology opens borders, educational and professional exchanges open minds." Institute of International Education (IIE), New York, www.iie.org.

Global Leadership Education at Handong

Global Education and Leadership

$\mathcal{W}$e are experiencing one of the most significant changes that we have ever experienced in recent history, a kind of global seismic shift in human history. As we get deeper into the 21st century, the advancement in cutting-edge science and technology is bringing an accelerated globalization to every aspect of our lives. We have entered the global age. In this ever-shrinking globe, we are rapidly becoming global citizens; i.e., we are living and working in a rapidly changing global environment. This globalization has caused consolidation among various parochial and localized views and ideologies; i.e., convergence among many splintering local economic and social forces, among differing challenges and opportunities, among contradictory interests and commitments, among diversified values and tastes, and among various environmental issues, to name only a few. Thinking and working globally will be critical for survival and prosperity in this century for all mankind sharing one globe. As global citizens, we are required to develop a global mind-set; i.e., increase our capacity to think and work on a global and intercultural basis. This can be accomplished through new higher education that meets the challenges of the 21st century.

The globalization of Handong aims to follow the Great Commission of our Lord Jesus Christ. *"Go into all the world and preach the Good News to everyone, everywhere" (Mark16:15).* The Lord also gave us two great commandments — *"Love God with all your heart, with all your soul, and with all your mind"* and *"Love your neighbor as you love yourself" (Matt.22:37-39).* Through globalization, we Christians have ample opportunities to interact with one another on a worldwide scale. But we must comprehend the bigger picture of God's universal plan to find our calling in the reformation of the world for Christ and His Kingdom.

The three important components of global leadership education are global communication ability, global professional ability, and global character. Since its inception in 1995, the mission of Handong is aimed at educating honest and competent future global leaders who will transform and serve communities, nations, and the world through professional capability and morality.

Education for the "Unknown"

We moved from a Newtonian physical world of the industrial age to an Einstein's quantum physical chaotic world of the information age.[26] Newtonian physics is based on the principle of cause and effect, of predictability and certainty, of distinct wholes and parts, of reality being what is actually seen. Newtonian physics is science of quantifiable determinism of linear thinking and of a controllable future as the result of the new approach to solving problems, the so-called analytical method. It is a world that does not change too fast or in unexpected ways.

But we now live in a time of chaos, rich in potential for new possibilities defying our traditional sense. A new world is being born. We need new ideas, new ways of seeing, and new relationships to help each other. Quantum physics at the subatomic level is changing our understanding of how the world works. The quantum universe is a world of chaos and process involving intertwined matter, energy, space, and time, not just of objects and things. Quantum physics does not speak of definite locations, speed, and paths of quanta. Instead, it speaks of probability and chances.

The Change of Academic Content for the 21st Century

In the 21st century, the content of academic education must undergo a fundamental change. During the industrialized period of the 20th century, hardware-centered standardized products were mass-produced and their production level was an important indicator of a country's wealth. University education during that period was geared to train students to memorize much of the contents in textbooks, and such knowledge was useful for a long time during one's working career.

However, education should not stop at memorization. Education should teach students how to explore the unknown, challenge the impossible, and have the ability to be creative. The 21st century is characterized by software-centered, smaller volume, highly customized product production. In the information era, the rate of change of knowledge is fast, and the life cycle of new information and knowledge, especially in technical fields, is short, fast, and explosive. The knowledge gained from textbooks in schools becomes obsolescent quickly. Memorization-based education should be drastically curtailed.[27]

Handong's approach is to encourage students to explore "new knowledge with no answers as yet" and help them to acquire abilities to think critically and to solve problems creatively. We must move away from uniform, all-encompassing education, which attempts to teach students memory-based information in all academic fields at an average, mediocre level. New information and knowledge are growing and dying out at a breathtaking rate. "Spoon-feeding" education based on memorization can no longer keep pace with the change. Handong must develop specialized education that challenges students to gain a comprehensive understanding of relevant academic disciplines and the relationships among them, while making the best of individual students' special talents and strengths.

Transdisciplinary Education

The new challenge facing global leadership education is to impart broad knowledge that transcends the barriers of academic disciplines. The academic departments in universities have traditionally been established along the dividing lines of academic fields. But, the problems and challenges in today's world do not occur along the lines of academic disciplines. For example, an accident in a steel mill is not just a problem in metallurgy, but also a complex problem involving mechanical, electrical, and electronic engineering, as well as operational management. Therefore, a solution for the problem requires a broad knowledge and know-how in all relevant technical fields.

To educate future global leaders, today's university education must emphasize interdisciplinary and transdisciplinary education that network among various academic fields. For example, networking among business, technology, and law becomes important. Since the advancement in technology has accelerated globalization of business, an interdisciplinary program has been created to fill the gap between business and technology. It is based on the recognition that business and technology cannot operate by themselves and that the two are interdependent on each other in the globalizing world.

Whole Person Moral and Ethical Education

In solving complex problems in the global context, it is not sufficient for future global leaders to be well prepared only in academic and technical fields. They must be trained to think and act with global leadership qualities. Another challenge for education is that universities must provide global leadership training and education, which combines academic and technical education with training in business ethics, social responsibility, environmental protection, and a mutually beneficial cooperative perspective. Above all, future global leaders must be honest, trustworthy, and truly dependable.

University education faces a real challenge in offering effective character development education, combined with practical experience in social service and international cooperation, global communication ability, and competent professional capability. Multidisciplinary knowledge is essential for competent leadership with both capability and character, but true leadership is founded on the character education of honesty and integrity. Honesty is the best policy and is the universal foundation for changing and serving the world. Character is the first priority for global leadership growth.

Handong adheres to an extensive honor code of ethics which deals with many aspects of academic and community life. Handong adopted non-proctored examinations as honesty training when it opened in 1995, and this now has become a precious tradition. The Handong Honor Code inculcates responsibility, diligence, service, sacrifice, and dignity in students' daily lives. Handong's students hold a purity pledge ceremony, which is a student-initiated movement. They have pledged to keep purity of spirit, mind, and body before God. Their character education includes cooperative living through residence halls, teamwork, social awareness, and the spirit of service to communities.

See Globally and Act Globally

Handong's arena was global since its beginning in 1995. That globalization was aimed at fulfilling the Great Commission of our Lord Jesus Christ, *"Go into the entire world and preach the good news to all creations" (Mark 16:15).* The goal of Handong is to equip its students with knowledge, character, and Christian faith that they need in order to provide global leadership throughout the world. Becoming global leaders requires an ability to communicate globally and to understand other cultures. It requires a global mind-set to view the entire world as the main domain for all educational and professional activities.

It is said that about 80 percent of the unevangelized people in the world live in Asia, people who have never heard of the love of God through Jesus Christ. Our Lord said *"And this gospel of the kingdom will be preached in the whole world as a testimony to all nations, and then the end will come" (Matt. 24:14).* Given its geographical advantage and cultural affinity for evangelizing the developing nations of Asia, Korea is strategically positioned to fulfill the mission.

Now, at the 10-year mark, God's command to me, which was to lead a university founded on His plan and purpose, has become a reality, despite the devastating financial crises and suffering that has been involved. Many people wondered what would become of Handong. When faced with severe difficulties and opposition, I had to live out the words of Rev. Oral Roberts, founder of Oral Roberts University.[19] *"When you see the invisible, you can do the impossible" (Hebrews 11:27).* Had I not done so, I would not have been able to envision this beautiful university campus and stately buildings, our wonderful students, and the devoted Christian professors and staff. These would have seemed impossible.

During this period, God allowed me to be tested beyond my strength, but my faith has grown through these difficulties. It has been proved over and over again that all the tests and hardships have been for the purpose of strengthening my faith and transforming Handong. Today, more than 20,000 devout Christians in Korea and abroad are supporting and praying for Handong. People are aware that it is established and functioning despite the lack of a wealthy foundation, benefactor, or denomination behind it, and it is for that reason that they have called Handong "God's University." God has been its foundation and benefactor. God's grace and guidance have been provided to us like manna in the wilderness.

In this 21st century, we, Christians, are asked more than ever to be conscious of our brothers and sisters in all nations on earth. God has raised up Handong to be an effective channel for training Christian men and women that He can use globally.

God has given Handong a global mission to restore shattered bonds of academia and enlarge His Kingdom through holistic education for the 21st century.

The late Father Reuben Archer Torrey III, who founded Jesus Abby in Korea in 1964, said that he had been praying for the establishment of a genuine Christian university in Korea. He recited the two following Bible verses:

"Your people (HGU) will rebuild the ancient ruins and will raise up the old-aged foundation, and you will be called the repairer of the broken walls, and restorer of streets with dwellings" (Isaiah 58:12).

"This city (HGU) will bring me renown, joy, praise, and honor before all nations on earth that hear of all good things I do for it: and they will be in awe and tremble at the abundant prosperity and peace I provide for it" (Jeremiah 33:9).

Before our Lord Jesus Christ ascended to heaven, He commanded us, *"Go and make disciples of all nations, baptizing them in the name of the Father and of the Son and of the Holy Spirit, and teaching them to obey every-*

thing I have commanded you. And surely I am with you always, to the very end of the age" (Matt. 28:19, 20).

Just as Western missionaries helped Korea in the 19th century, now it is our turn to serve our fellow people of Asia in the 21st century. In spreading the gospel, Korea is obligated to the unreached nations in Asia.

Enlarge the Site of Your Tent

So far, international students from as many as 59 nations have come to study at Handong. The international joint MBA program of Handong with the Institute of Finance and Economics (IFE) in Ulaanbaatar, Mongolia, started in 1999. As of 2005, some 50 Mongolian graduates from this joint program are working at various Mongolian government agencies, multinational companies, banks, and universities. I feel rewarded when we receive positive feedback from our graduates who state that the program has helped them work more effectively. From 2006, this joint program will be co-sponsored by UNESCO as part of their UNESCO/UNITWIN Network program.

In September 2003, Handong concluded an agreement with the Ministry of Higher and Secondary Specialized Education of Uzbekistan and Tashkent State University of Economics to establish a joint MBA program there. In August 2005, HGU made an agreement to conduct a training program for young Uzbek teachers in cooperation with the government of Uzbekistan. The program will encourage the participants to acquire practical and updated pedagogical skills to bring out talents endowed in their students.

Our cooperation with developing countries also includes Afghanistan. In April 2003, Handong made an agreement with the Afghan Ministry of Higher Education and Kandahar University to support their development efforts. Utilizing summer vacation time, Handong professors and students visit Afghanistan to teach IT, business, and industrial design at Kandahar University.

In 2005, Handong established the ASIA RESEARCH INSTITUTE of LANGUAGE AND CULTURE (ARILAC) in cooperation with GBT (Global Bible Translator), WBT (Wycliffe Bible Translators), and SIL (Summer Institute of Linguistics), to educate missionaries via Bible translation in unreached nations. Graduate students of this program come from Korea as well as overseas.

As I witness the international cooperation that is taking place, I see how God uses Handong to spread His love around the globe. *"And how can they preach unless they are sent? As it is written, 'How beautiful are the feet of those who bring good news!'" (Romans 10:15).*

A Dream for International Law School Realized

I had several God-given global visions, one of them being a dream to establish Handong International Law School (HILS). I began to share my dream with others and talked about the need for Korea as well as other developing countries to produce international lawyers to expand their markets in the global community.

Since Korea joined the Organization for Economic Cooperation and Development (OECD), Korea's legal market will open to the world and legal issues involving international parties will grow. Korea is receiving an ever-increasing demand for professionals in the fields of international law and trade, yet there is a dire shortage of international legal professionals in Korea now. We must establish an international law school based on the U.S. law school system and cultivate international law professionals who can work on the global stage.

One day in 2000, U.S. attorney S.K. Lee from Chicago, the grandfather of Handong's English service pastor, visited

HGU. I said to him, "Attorney Lee, won't you come and work with us at Handong?"

From that time on, Attorney Lee worked passionately to make the International Law School a reality. Finally in 2002, the Ministry of Education of Korea approved the Graduate School of Handong International Law School (HILS), which is, indeed, the first American-style law school in Asia. Later, through the introduction of Pastor Billy Kim, the former chairman of the Baptist World Alliance, I invited Professor Lynn Buzzard, then of Campbell University Law School in North Carolina, to be the chartered Dean of HILS. As an attorney and a pastor, he had worked not only with U.S. law firms, but also had advised governments of various Asian countries on their constitutions. He also founded the Christian Legal Society (CLS) in the United States, which impacted the legal environment in that country. What is amazing is that he had been praying for a law school that would produce Christian lawyers. HILS was the answer to his prayers!

The Chartered Dean of HILS, Lynn Buzzard

At the third admissions ceremony for HILS in 2004, Ambassador Thomas C. Hubbard, the then U.S. Ambassador to Korea, honored us with his presence. HILS attracted much interest and attention from educational circles and international societies. As of 2005, students from over 18 countries are studying at HILS, which offers full scholarship to students from developing countries. So far, 15 students passed the U.S. bars (Tennessee, New York). If a dream is conceived, it is realized in due time.

In 2004, the largest international seminar in Handong's history took place on campus. It was co-sponsored by the Ministry of Education and the Korean Educational Development Institute (KEDI) and was supported by Handong as well as the World Bank and OECD. Guest speakers, including Dr. Jamil Salmi, Manager of the Educational Section of the World Bank, and Dr. Carl Dahlman of the World Bank Institute, complimented HGU on its pioneering spirit to launch HILS and the progress Handong has made in less than a decade.

A New Cross-Disciplinary Global Leadership-MBA

Global Leadership-MBA, which integrates technology, business, and law, is the world's first cross-disciplinary higher education, conducted by Handong Global University. Handong opened the first International Law School in 2002 in Asia and is in a unique position to offer the Global Leadership-MBA. This program is highly desirable in the blurred age of the 21st century.

Educational Philosophy of the Global Leadership-MBA

The basic concept of the Global Leadership-MBA is depicted below.

Figure 1 Change of Technology, Business and Law over Time
(From Isolation in the 20th century to Integration in the 21st century)

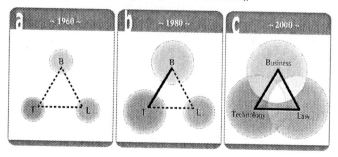

Change of Technology, Business, and Law over Time

In the industrial era of the 1950s, technology, business, and law disciplines were largely separate and unrelated while their domains were small as shown in Fig 1a above. As technology advanced in the '80s, the domain of technology and that of resulting business grew although the interaction between technology and law still remained very little or intermittent, at best, as shown in Fig 1b. In the information and knowledge-driven global world of the 21st century, however, the domains of technology, business, and law have greatly expanded — to the extent that the three overlap and intersect as seen in Fig 1c above. Finally, the three intersecting circles became a tight crystalline structure, forming a ruggedly interlocked and comprehensive knowledge structure that is vital for true global leadership in the new century. The same can be said for the educational philosophy of the

Global Leadership-MBA. It offers a combined discipline of the three essential elements that form a tight crystalline, as illustrated further below.

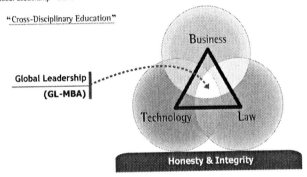

Figure 2 Educational Concept for "Global Leadership - MBA"

Global Leadership-MBA Integrating Technology, Business, and Law, Based upon Honesty and Integrity

It is not the intent of the Global Leadership-MBA Program to turn the students into experts in specific areas of various disciplines, but rather to equip them to effectively function as generalists with insights into specific areas. The ultimate goal is to enable them to apply interdisciplinary and transdisciplinary skills to integrate and synthesize the various related areas and arrive at common goals and objectives for the common good of all constituent elements concerned.

Business transactions in this global and competitive world necessarily involve broad knowledge of advanced and emerging technologies as well as of law. Indeed, keeping pace with the speed and flow of information that global leaders have to cope with begins with the capacity to comprehend current and future technological advances in the global arena.

In global multinational businesses, interaction between business and law, including international businesses and trade, mergers and acquisitions, etc., becomes significant, and carries much more weight now. These needs prompted several U.S. universities to offer joint educational degree programs combining the MBA and JD. A higher educational program combining business and technology has also been tried as Techno-MBA degrees in several U.S. universities.

On the other hand, the interaction of technology and laws for subjects such as intellectual property, IT laws, cyberspace laws, etc., is also intensifying and becoming critical in our technology-driven global world. Able global leaders of modern days must be familiar with the rules of law, treaties, conventions, laws and regulations that govern national and international relationships, and must be able to deal with contracts and trade regulations as well as intellectual property rights. An astute global leader must have broad knowledge of "the big picture" integrating technology, business, and law spanning the globe.

The Vital Character Education in the Global Leadership-MBA

Global leadership also requires both capability and good character. Multidisciplinary knowledge is essential for competent leadership combined with both capability and character, but true leadership is founded on character education of honesty and integrity. Honesty is the best policy, and character is the first priority for global leadership growth.

The educational concept of the Handong's Global Leadership-MBA is based on a holistic approach combining professional training with ethical and character education. Handong has a strong passion for the total education of the whole person for the Global-MBA which will result in global and true prosperity in the world.

Handong envisions the Global Leadership-MBA Program to provide the students with foundational training in character building and insight in leadership. The Global Leadership-MBA curriculum must be designed to expose the students to world history and the great ideas of historical figures of high moral and ethical character, as well as provide opportunities for the students to become competent leaders with passionate commitments for the betterment of mankind for the people they serve.

Along with the Global Leadership-MBA Program, another initiative at Handong is the Global Institute for Ideas and Innovation (GIII), an institute and think tank that aims to extend these concepts and link them to actual businesses and industries. One of its goals is to help students apply what they have learned in school to actual businesses and to train them to set up their own enterprises. Another very important goal is to supervise international students, who plan to work in IT industries when they return to their home countries, so that they may leapfrog along their path to catch up with the developed countries. I profess that all of these dreams are entirely from God. As always, God provided the means and tools to bring them to life. He sent workers with the right skills and talents for the projects precisely when they were needed. Time after time, I witnessed that the Lord is the best project manager and He is the master of just-in-time management.

"Enlarge the place of your tent, stretch your tent curtains wide, do not hold back; lengthen your cords, strengthen your stakes. For you will spread out to the right and to the left; your descendants will dispossess nations and settle in their desolate cities" (Isaiah 54:2-3).

Global Partnership for Peace and Prosperity in the 21st Century

Dinner Speech for the Students from the John F. Kennedy
School of Government
HARVARD UNIVERSITY
by
President Young-Gil Kim of HANDONG GLOBAL
UNIVERISTY
April 1, 2006
Held at Seoul Plaza Hotel, Korea

Good Evening!!
On behalf of Handong Global University, I would like to welcome the students from the JFK School of Government, Harvard University. I am very delighted and excited that students from the JFK School of Government and Handong International Law School (HILS) are meeting together. It is important for you to get to know each other and form a network since I believe you will become leaders of the next generation.

I want to take this opportunity to give you a brief background and the founding educational philosophy of Handong Global University and also share with you one of Handong's visions. Handong's vision is to build a global network of the leaders who will work together to achieve global prosperity and peace. The reason why I say *global* prosperity and peace rather than limiting them to Korea or to one particular nation is because of the fact that we no longer live in a world where we are isolated from one another. The world has become so closely knitted together that one nation's peace and prosperity are directly linked to those of the rest. Therefore, it is Handong's primary goal to educate and train global leaders for tomorrow. Through this meeting, I want you to be challenged by Handong's global vision and take part in it as future leaders of America.

Handong Global University opened its doors for higher education in 1995 in Pohang, located on the southeastern coast of Korea. As the name signifies, Handong Global University was established from the very beginning with a founding focus to become a *global* university that would impact not only Korea, but also other countries on the globe as well. The academic mission of Handong is aimed at training ordinary students to become exceptional leaders who are competent and who have high credibility suited for this global, technology-driven market place of the 21st century. Our goal is to educate not only students in Korea, but also those from countries that have a substandard educational system or who need assistance from others.

Handong has a motto for the purpose of challenging and reminding the students of our founding focus which is, "Why Not Change the World?" One of Handong's new influential vehicles to achieve such a goal was the establishment of Handong International Law School, or HILS, in 2002. This law school serves as an international law school focusing not only on the laws of the United States, but also of other Asian countries. As true leaders of the future, it is essential that we be familiar with the laws of other countries, for such knowledge will form the building blocks of communication and collaboration with them. Without comprehending other countries' judicial systems, one cannot fully serve as a global leader.

Currently, students from more than 30 countries are studying at Handong including Afghanistan, Australia, Brazil, Burundi, Canada, Cambodia, Cameroon, China, Germany, England, Haiti, Hungary, India, Indonesia, Israel, Japan, Jordan, Malaysia, Mongolia, New Zealand, North Korea, Philippines, Russia, Saudi Arabia, South Africa, Swaziland, Thailand, Tunisia, Uganda, United States, Uzbekistan, and Vietnam. The students from developing countries are mostly on a full scholarship and our primary focus is to educate them so that when they return to their respective countries, they may serve as leaders and have beneficial impact on their countries. Currently, international students comprise only 5 percent of the whole of Handong's student body, but our goal is to increase it up to 20 percent in the next five years. The primary reason why we invite and provide international students with scholarships and take the time to educate them is to help bring up the living standards of the whole world. It is time to stop focusing on the development and wealth only of individual countries, but to promote the cause for all countries to prosper together, that is, to prosper globally.

Let me provide you with some real live examples of how Handong has been able to reach out to some of those countries and realize its goal of cultivating future leaders who will change the world.

Handong started a joint MBA program with the Institute of Finance and Economics (IFE) at Ulaanbaatar in Mongolia in 1999. Handong signed an agreement of cooperation with the Ministry of Higher Education, Afghanistan, and Kandahar University to develop an educational exchange program in April 2003. Handong has been sending faculty and students to Afghanistan to teach computer skills each summer. Handong also signed an agreement with the Ministry of Higher and Secondary Specialized Education of Uzbekistan and Tashkent State University of Economics for the establishment of a joint MBA program in September of 2003. An agreement of cooperation between the "ISTEDOD" Foundation of Uzbekistan, Tashkent University of Economics was also established.

These are some of the examples of how Handong has been reaching out to other countries and assisting them to bring up the quality of their education. However, as you may already know, it is not possible to achieve the goal on our own, alone. We must form a web of alliances among the schools that share the same vision. I want to invite you — students from the JFK School of Harvard — to share with us our vision of the changing the world. Forming partnerships with you will create even stronger networks to provide assistance to countries in needs. More importantly, you, as leaders of the next generation, will be able to bring about global prosperity and peace, which will make this world a better place to live for *all* of us, and for our children, for many generations to come. Thank you!!

Epilogue

$\mathcal{H}$andong's history is truly a story of tears and joy. Handong was like a small child whose mother ran out of milk. Yet, it has been able to stand before God and our society despite all the trials — all because of His amazing providence, grace, and touch.

God guided this school of the wilderness in miraculous ways over the past years, and along the way, He trained us as His disciples. Thus, our students and professors call Handong *God's School* without any reservation. Our pains were great and unbearable at times, but He has also given us precious gifts along the way. The gifts are the Handong students, who proudly wear their caps and gowns on graduation day. I am overjoyed when I receive news that our graduates have been accepted by U.S. Ivy League universities, including Harvard, Yale, and Columbia, to further their studies. I feel rewarded when I hear that Handong's graduates have started working at UN organizations and many multinational companies, such as IBM, Intel, Cisco, and Microsoft. I am proud when I hear others praising the quality of our graduates.

My heart trembles as I imagine how these graduates will impact their countries and societies, and I cannot wait to hear stories of how they serve as leaders and role models in their own countries when they go back after finishing their studies. Their potential is the true worth and cause of joy that we experience every day at this school of the wilderness. Chapter 29 of the Book of Acts in the Bible continues here at Handong in our 21st century!

I sincerely pray that Handong educates and sends out Christian leaders who will change the world in this century. However, reaching this goal has been an arduous task, requiring emptying and lowering of ourselves. Henri J.M. Nouwen said in his book, *In the Name of Jesus — Reflections on Christian Leadership*,[29] "The way of the Christian leader is not the way of upward mobility in which our world has invested so much, but the way of downward mobility, ending on the cross. It is not a leadership of power and control, but a leadership of powerless and humility in which the suffering servant of God, Jesus Christ, is made manifest. The power is constantly abandoned in favor of love. It is a true spiritual leadership."

There are two great laws operating in this universe: the law of gravitation in the visible, physical world, and the law of grace in the invisible, spiritual world. The law of gravity governs the movement of the material world and is restricted to the earth, while the law of grace, which dominates the spiritual world, is bound for heaven. The law of gravity is earth-centered, while the law of grace is God-centered. The grace of which Philip Yancey writes in his book, *What's So Amazing About Grace?*[30], is the freely given and unmerited favor and love of God. The main purpose of life for non-Christians is to enlarge the gravitational field by maximizing the force of gravity in pursuit of the material riches in the visible world. But true Christian leadership requires giving up one's visible things and pursuing the invisible things in the spiritual world. By giving up the visible things in the material world, one gains invisible things in the spiritual world and can change the world in return. Handong students say, "Let's study hard and give it away for others to transform the world." By being able to see what they can gain in the spiritual world, they can readily give away the visible things as needed to change the visible world.

Handong's history is, indeed, a pilgrim's progress because it is the realization of God's plan to spread the Gospel to the ends of the remaining world. For that purpose, He chose a nameless, debt-ridden, frail institution with a totally uncertain future rather than a rich and famous university, many of which abound in the world, just as He chose to send Jesus, our savior, as a carpenter born in a lowly manger in a stable.

This book is only the first volume of the pilgrim's progress of Handong, and each new day in Handong's life sees another page written in the next volume. What we saw so far is only the tip of the iceberg of God's grand plan for the school. God is steering the iceberg and when the whole plan is finally revealed, that should be the day when His message reaches the ends of the world and His Great Commission is fulfilled.

"Our Lord and God, you are worthy to receive glory and honor and power, for you created all things, and by your will, they were created and have their being" (Revelation 4:11).

APPENDIX:
"Handong vs. Harvard"

Reflections of a Visiting Professor:
by
Charles W. Herman, Ph.D.
Professor of History
Department of History & Political Science, University of
Sioux Falls
Sioux Falls, South Dakota 57105, USA

*B*efore I arrived at Handong Global University in Pohang, Korea, in March 2005, I wondered what kind of academic realities I would find when I met my colleagues and students there. I had corresponded with the chairperson of the School of General Studies, the dean of Academic Affairs, and the Office of International Affairs. Everyone appeared to be helpful and knowledgeable, but I still wondered if the reality would match the appearance.

I was not disappointed. My students were as bright and enthusiastic as any I had taught in the U.S., and my colleagues were as dedicated and diligent as any I had ever known. But I still wondered about Handong's educational programs. What specific outcomes did the university wish to see? To what extent has the university achieved its mission — that is, does the curriculum really prepare leaders for the 21st century?

When I was searching for answers to questions such as these, I remembered reading about a plan at Harvard to revise its general education curriculum, and I decided to compare programs and objectives at the two universities. The results of this comparison were truly remarkable. In its short history, Handong has already established outcomes and programs that Harvard has only recently decided to emphasize. (A summary of Harvard's recommendations can be found at: www.fas.**harvard**.edu/curriculum-review/**Summary**_of_ Recs.pdf.).

Perhaps a few examples from the Harvard report will demonstrate this finding.

- **Internationalizing the Curriculum**
  The Harvard report says: "We recommend that we enhance significantly the opportunities for our students in international studies … [an area] in which the world has changed most dramatically since our last general review of the undergraduate curriculum. … Every Harvard College student should be expected to complete an international experience, defined as study, research, or work abroad, and — no matter their level of proficiency upon entering Harvard — continue studying a foreign language." This is an area where Handong excels. From teaching foreign languages, especially English and Chinese, to recruiting international students and sending Handong students to study and live outside Korea, Handong has programs that help students to see the world from a global perspective. In this respect, Handong is already doing what Harvard is planning to do in the future.

- **Choosing an Academic Major**
  The Harvard report recommends that "the timing of concentration [major] choice, which now takes place in the freshman year, should be delayed to the middle of the sophomore year. A later timing of concentration choice . . . would provide students greater opportunities for intellectual exploration before committing to in-depth work in a concentration."
  Handong has adopted a similar policy already. In addition, Harvard recommends reducing the size of academic majors so that students will be able to explore more widely a variety of academic disciplines and approaches to knowledge. To achieve these same outcomes at Handong, students are expected to acquire knowledge in adjoining fields that will supplement and support their academic majors.

- **Building a Sense of Community**
  The Harvard report says: "To build a strong sense of community at Harvard College, we recommend that freshmen be assigned to their upper-class House upon arrival."
  Most Handong students reside on campus. For this reason, the university functions practically as a self-contained community. Students study together, eat and live together, pray and play together. Because students share time, space, and experiences so intimately, they also learn how to share responsibilities, participate in group activities, cooperate, help, support, and serve each other. Skills and dispositions such as these will not appear on their Handong transcripts, but they are just as important for leaders and workers in the 21st century as any

other set of qualifications (both in the church and in secular society).

- ## Building Relationships Between Instructors and Students

  The Harvard report recommended smaller classes and a small group seminar during the first year because, the Harvard panel said, "We recognize that a liberal education is, above all, a shared endeavor of students and faculty."

  The Handong faculty is a wonderful asset for Handong because they love the university, their academic vocations, and their students. While it is not unusual for professors to love their research, their academic disciplines, and the ambience of university life, many have only limited contact with their students. If instructors work at research universities, for example, they must devote much time to their research projects, and they may have little time left for students. Instruction at research universities is often provided by teaching assistants, not full-time and tenured professors. At Handong, however, faculty do more than work on research projects. They also teach, counsel, and mentor students. They pray and worship with students during Wednesday chapel services. They may eat with students in the cafeteria or at the campus restaurant, and most full-time instructors meet weekly with a team of about 25 students. Again, it is apparent that Handong has realized already an outcome that Harvard is only hoping to achieve.

Similarities such as these show that Handong's mission is actively progressive, and its vision for higher education is shared by one of the most prestigious universities in the world. While we may be impressed by similarities such as these, there are also some obvious and revealing differences between Handong and Harvard. For example, the Harvard report contained no references to spiritual values, computer or IT skills, a commitment to diversity, integration of faith and learning, service projects, and appreciation for the disposition of servanthood. Emphases such as these are central to Handong's mission and design for higher education, and especially its focus on character development and spiritual values.

By making these comparisons, I am not suggesting that Handong is in the same class with Harvard. Nevertheless, I think it is important to celebrate what Handong has achieved in its brief history of only 10 years — or to state the case in Handong's own unique way, "to celebrate what God has done at Handong."

References

1. *Know What You Believe*, by Paul E. Little, (1970), Chariot Victor Publisher
2. *Evidence That Demands a Verdict*, by Josh McDowell, (1972), Thomas Nelson
3. *The Liberation of Planet Earth*, by Hal Lindsey, (1974), Zondervan
4. *Scientific Creationism*, by Henry M. Morris, (1974), Master Books Inc.
5. *What is Creation Science?*, by Henry M. Morris and Gary E. Parker, (1982), Master Books
6. *Evolution: The Fossils Still Say No!*, by Duane T. Gish, (1976), Creative Life Publishers
7. *The Illustrated Origins Answers Book*, by P.S. Taylor, (1995), Eden Communications
8. *Darwin on Trial*, by Phillip E. Johnson, (1993), InterVarsity Press
9. *How Now Shall We Live?*, by Charles Colson and N. Pearcey, (1999), LifeWay Press
10. *The Case for Faith*, by Lee Strobel, (2000), by Zondervan
11. *The Wedge of Truth*, by Phillip E. Johnson, (2000), InterVarsity Press
12. *The Purpose Driven Life*, by Rick Warren, (2002), Zondervan

13. *Rumors of Another World,* by Philip Yancey, (2003), Zondervan
14. *Finding God in the Questions,* by Timothy Johnson, (2004), InterVarsity Press
15. *Good Life,* by Charles Colson, (2005), Tyndale House
16. *Is That Really You, God?,* by Loren Cunningham, (1984), YWAM Publishing
17. *Daring to Live on the Edge,* by Loren Cunningham, (1991), YMAM Publishing
18. *Rees Howells: Intercessor,* by Norman Grubb, (1997), CLC Publications
19. *Oral Roberts: Still Doing the Impossible,* (2002), Destiny Image
20. *Chemical Evolution and Origin of Life,* (1971), p.320, American Elsevier
21. *Principles of Biochemistry,* by A. Lehninger, (1983), p.179, New York: Worth Publisher
22. *Nature,* "Hoyle on Evolution," by Fred Hoyle, November 12, (1981), p.105
23. *Newsweek,* Science News, November 3 (1980)
24. *A Tale of Three Kings: a Study in Brokenness,* by Gene Edwards, (1992), Tyndale House
25. *Lessons from the Future: Making Sense of a Blurred World from the World's Leading Futurist,* by Stan Davis, (2001), Capstone Publishing
26. *Global Leaders for the 21ˢᵗ Century,* by Michael J. Marquardt and Nancy O. Berger, (2000), SUNY Press
27. *History of Education in America,* by J.D. Pulliam, (1994), Merril
28. *Engaging God's World,* by Cornelius Plantinga Jr., (2002), Eerdmans Publishing Co.
29. *In the Name of Jesus,* by Henri J.M. Nouwen, (1989), Crossroad Publishing
30. *What's So Amazing about Grace?,* by Philip Yancey, (2002), Zondervan

PAPYRUS BASKET

Do you remember the papyrus basket that housed Moses?
Handong Global University is like the papyrus basket.
As Moses — housed in the papyrus basket — was later used
  as God's man
to save the world's races (Exodus 2:3),
Handong students will be the future leaders who change the
  world.

Handong Global University, as God's university, wants to be
  the papyrus basket
which will produce God's people who will save all nations.
In a time when many feel desperate that there is little hope
  in this world,
we have hope because of Handong Global University
for we have God, the dream that He gave us, and the precious
  students that He sent us.

In this world ill with ethical and spiritual decay,
we need prayers and participation of those who want God
and await for the birth of God's University.
But the new history through Handong cannot be realized
  without your prayers and support.
Handong would like to invite you to be our partners of the
  Papyrus Basket.

****

Handong International Foundation (HIF) is a tax-exempt, nonprofit organization under the tax code 501(c)(3) with the following address:

HIF
c/o Rev. Jong-Yong Lee, chairman of HIF
Cornerstone Church
24428 S. Vermont Avenue
Harbor City, California 90710
Tel : (310) 530-4040
Fax : (310) 530-8400
E-mail: lahandong@hotmail.com
Handong Global University: www.handong.edu

Printed in the United States
55482LVS00003B/8